CRIES FROM THE CORRIDOR

The New Suburban Ghettos
PETER McLAREN

❶ METHUEN

Toronto   New York   London   Sydney

Canadian Cataloguing in Publication Data

McLaren, Peter, 1948-
  Cries from the corridor

ISBN 0-458-94450-5 bd. ISBN 0-458-94340-1 pa.

1. McLaren, Peter, 1948- 2. Teachers—Ontario
—Toronto—Biography. I. Title.

LA2325.M26A3 372.11'0092'4 C80-094094-6

Cover design: Brant Cowie
Back cover photo: Barbara Wilde

Printed and bound in Canada

1 2 3 4 5 80 84 83 82 81

To my wife, Jenny

Acknowledgements

I would like to thank Victor Schwartzman and Pat Banning for their constant encouragement and editorial assistance with the manuscript, and a particular thanks to Murray Spence for his wise counsel.

A special word of thanks is due Dr. Fred Rainsberry and Dr. Laurier LaPierre for their moral support in this project.

I also wish to express my deepest gratitude to Jim Montgomerie, Canada's maverick educator, and Ron Beattie for enabling me to grow as a teacher. Also, as administrators, they encouraged me to be myself—something rare in education today.

Contents

There are millions of children around the world with emotional problems. In Canada alone, of a population of ten million children, one million suffer emotional distress.

Most of them are not born with these problems. They develop them as they are growing up. They learn to be sick. They are reacting to situations that exist in their environment: parents, schools and society at large.

The incidents in this book are based on part of my four and a half years of teaching. While I have changed the names and some details to avoid embarrassment to others, what you are about to read is not fiction. It is the day-to-day facts of an inner-city teacher's life.

... Ontario ... a place worthy of all the things this province stands for ... a place where children get first consideration, because we're a young province, and children are our most important resource. ...

Part of the text of a film, *A Place to Stand*, spoken by Premier William Davis at Cinesphere, Ontario Place, Toronto.

Foreword

The Corridor of which Peter McLaren speaks is everywhere; geographically it exists in all the provinces of Canada. It is impossible to avoid it, and those who close their eyes as they walk through it quickly do so at their own peril.

Perhaps you will share some of my emotions as the universe of some of our children unfolds before you in these pages.

My first emotion was one of horror. We live in a benign country, in the last quarter of the twentieth century. Our standard of living is one of the highest in the world and our national sense of responsibility is well documented. Why then have we as citizens allowed the Corridor to be erected? It is hard to plead ignorance.

My second emotion was anger—at the bureaucrats, the experts, the journalists. Here is a group of children being brought up in what amounts to a jungle within the walls of a city of my country. Why was I not told?

Then I felt disgust at those who preach fiscal restraint in the financial management of our schools, at those who refuse the educator the freedom to deal with all aspects of human life.

Slowly my feelings turned to apprehension and anxiety. What is going to happen to Peter McLaren's children? Will they ever emerge from the Corridor in which society has placed them? Will they ever cease to be the victims of the unconcern and manipulation of others? And, above all, how can they grow, develop, mature in the environment in which Peter McLaren has found them and in which we keep them? To save the children may well become the most elementary social priority of these last two decades of the twentieth century.

Then I experienced a sense of relief and gratitude—for Peter McLaren, a teacher and a person.

As a teacher, Peter McLaren knows the parameters of his job. Yet he tests them and goes beyond them. He understands the needs of children and reconciles his needs with theirs. He has a respect for their individuality and a concern for their physical well-being. His training and his humanity meet in the crucible of experience, and joy and fulfillment become possible and realizable. We can have sociological studies on the one hand or we can be grateful to hear from one who has lived in the midst of it, telling us as it is.

Every page of this book attests to Peter McLaren's determination to learn and reach beyond the confines of himself, to adapt to the living of what is both a nightmare and a revelation.

If you look about you, you will find that there are many Peter McLarens—they inhabit our schools unheralded, often molested and frequently judged harshly. Yet every day, they *do* and *are*.

There has been no other statement on "our schools" that will help as much to clarify the situation, document the case, and elicit a response as Peter McLaren's touching experiences.

Laurier La Pierre
January, 1980

Introduction

"Teach in an inner-city school! You're completely crazy," a friend warned me. "You'll ruin your career!"

I was taken aback. "What do you mean 'ruin my career?'"

"When you've decided you've had enough, and apply for a job in a better area, you'll be labelled an 'inner-city' teacher. Once you've been pigeon-holed as teaching mainly immigrant kids, you've had it. Be smart—get out before you get in."

But I wanted to work with inner-city kids and jobs were scarce.

The Jane-Finch Corridor is a six-square block area in the city of North York, a suburb just outside downtown Toronto. In 1970, there were twenty-one high-rise apartment buildings, and a population of 34,000. By 1975, there were fifty-nine high-rises (with four more under construction) and a population of sixty thousand. Almost half the people in the Jane-Finch Corridor are under nineteen.

Most inhabitants of the "Jane Jungle" live in government subsidized high-rises or townhouses. Most are new immigrants with low-paying jobs or no jobs at all. There is a substantial West Indian population, as well as Italian- and Spanish-speaking peoples.

Although the Jane-Finch Corridor is technically a suburb, it feels "inner-city" because of the large numbers of single-parent families, the low incomes, the high juvenile delinquency rate, the constant turnover in population, the government-subsidized housing, the high-density high-rise buildings.

When we think of inner-city schools, we visualize the ghettos of New York, London, Chicago, Detroit: the garbage-strewn streets, the smashed windows, the derelicts lying in doorways—whole sections of cities deserted in the rush to the suburbs. But in these new high-rise ghettos in the suburbs, with their facade of order and containment, conditions are beginning to parallel those horrors left behind in the cities.

There is crime and vandalism and racial tension. Police form "beat patrols" and special "youth squads." Shopping malls sprout up like fungi at major intersections. On weekends, low-income families organize into platoons to track down bargains.

The Corridor has one of the highest suicide rates in Metropolitan Toronto. The kids drink beer, smoke dope, shoot craps long into the night; they vandalize property and break into homes.

And they come to school. . . .

It's impossible to pin down the moment I decided I was going to be a teacher. Events leading to that decision occurred over a number of years, and only later was I able to link these experiences.

One of the reasons teaching appealed to me was because I couldn't imagine teachers stooping to the level of power politics. Teaching offered security, I believed, plus it held the attraction of actually inspiring and helping kids.

At sixteen I ruled out ever working for a large corporation when my father was fired as general manager of a large electronics firm. He had just turned fifty when the company's new owners decided to let out all the executives over forty-five; a month later he was fired. I watched my father try one low-paying job after another, a severe case of asthma finally forcing him into early retirement. After that, I vowed always to stay clear of the business world.

During my senior years in high school, I became disillusioned at how boring and pointless many of the lessons were. I was always fantasizing about standing in front of a class and teaching the most interesting lesson imaginable. With the arrogance of youth, I was sure I could do a better job at keeping students' interest.

As an only child in a protective middle-class family in the Toronto suburb of Willowdale, I led a fairly normal life as an above-average student during the week, and as a "weekend hippie" on Fridays and Saturdays.

When I finished high school, I had the itch to travel, so I decided to check out San Francisco, the mecca of "flower children." On the long bus ride to the west coast, I had my very first conversation with a black, a young radical who filled me in on the black scene in the States, an ugly picture. His unequivocal hatred of "whitey" made me extremely depressed.

Shortly after I arrived in San Francisco, an incident occurred that made me much more upset, even fearful. Walking alone in a deserted section of Golden Gate Park one afternoon, suddenly I was surrounded by a group of about a dozen blacks, kids no more than twelve, each brandishing weapons: knives, sticks, chains. Trembling, I pointed frantically to the tiny Canadian flag sewn on my knapsack: "I'm a Canadian. See? We aren't prejudiced, honestly!" The leader became confused: "Leave the mental alone." I was lucky. Afterwards, I comforted myself with the thought that in Canada we were immune to these problems.

For the next few years I shared a sixties' idealism that, somehow, Canada was a privileged place to be, and I still feel that way to a large extent. I assumed that we could handle any problem we were faced with through negotiation and education. After all, education seemed to be the most effective tool to shape our future. If we could fill our schools with "turned on" teachers, this "new breed" could swing things around: war could be abolished, the hungry fed and the poor found decent jobs. I looked at the racial problems in the States with a certain smugness; it could never happen in Canada, at least not with the right people in the system. I was full of hope for the future; a real and honest dialogue between adults and young people would bridge the generation gap.

When I graduated from university with a degree in English, I hung up my love beads, fatigue jacket and peace button, and a few months later got married. The following month I enrolled in Teacher's College, and in little over a year was hired to teach in a wealthy village just outside of Toronto.

Although I liked the kids and enjoyed teaching, something was missing; I felt expendable. These kids could get by in the world with probably any teacher; because of their background, they were almost assured success in the system. Working-class kids would be more of a challenge, I thought. Also, I wanted to enroll in graduate school in Toronto. Jenny, my wife, encouraged me to look for a job in the inner-city. "That's where you'll feel the most needed," she said. "They need young teachers in areas like that, with new ideas and a new approach." I handed in my resignation and began job-hunting.

My new principal told me he thought I'd made the right choice. He welcomed me to the ranks of inner-city teachers, leading me into his office saying, "Just call me Fred." I relaxed immediately.

In his mid-forties, he had a boyish grin and a thick shock of grey hair that looked strangely out of character. The button on his shirt read "I'm the boss." It was clear that the button was a joke. "The excellent grades I see in your Teacher's College report won't matter much here in the jungle," he began. "This is the real world." He leaned over the desk. "I only have one criterion for hiring new teachers. Every kid in this school, and I mean each one, has the right to be loved. No matter how difficult the kid is, no matter how he or she drives you batty from the very first day . . . give them all the love and affection you can. When it feels too impossible, come and see me and we'll talk. All right, Peter? Now good luck, and we'll see you in the morning."

I left his office with a good feeling. I later learned that he was somewhat of a folk legend in the city. As the "hugging principal," he had a fairly high success rate in creating an atmosphere of love and trust between teachers and students.

My tour of the school was conducted by Fred's secretary, who filled me in on all the latest school gossip as she led me past various classrooms, sketching portraits of the teachers inside. Usually, the reports were favourable, but there was always at least one complaint per teacher. When she remarked, "He always sends two of his kids down to the office with a pile of stencils to be run off late in the afternoon, when I'm busiest," I considered it a warning.

Later I ventured into the staff room. Several teachers were crammed into the tiny room, dutifully cleaning up the lunch dishes. A teacher was swearing at the broken coke machine; it had just eaten several quarters. "How do they manage to break into our staff room and screw up our coke machine?" he complained. "I thought the caretaker locked up after we leave!" He kicked the machine several times before finally giving up.

I introduced myself.

"We heard you were coming!" answered a voice near the sink. A big, rugged-looking man came over and introduced himself as the vice-principal, Rod. I shook his hand, which was still dripping with dishwater. "I suppose you'll manage just fine," he said, as he looked me over. "You've got youth on your side at least . . . doesn't he, John?" An elderly gentleman with a friendly smile came over and gave me a friendly pat on the shoulder. "Watch out for John," the vice-principal warned. "He's one of those health nuts! Maybe that's how he's lived so long!"

"Just keep yourself in shape and you'll survive, young man. Look how long I've lasted, and I've been at this game for over forty years!"

"Got any trade secrets?" I asked.

John grinned. "Sure! B-6!"

"B-6?" Suddenly, I felt stupid.

"B-6! Vitamin B-6! Good for the nerves, you know!"

I was hired to replace a teacher who couldn't handle the pressure. Her class comprised seventeen grade five students, and nineteen grade sixes, ranging in age from eleven to thirteen. This was a "regular" class, as opposed to "special" classes for kids with severe learning problems. As in most of the classes, a third of the students were black, most of them from the West Indies. I had never taught West Indian students before. Would they accept me?

They certainly hadn't accepted the teacher I was hired to replace. On one of her last days, all thirty-six students walked into her gym class, faced the far wall with their backs towards her, and refused to move. Several of the kids spit against the wall to punctuate their protest. I wasn't told why the kids were upset, and I decided not to ask.

My classroom was in a "portable" building, about fifty feet from the main building. It resembled one of those prefabricated units you see in a documentary film from World War Two. In fact, it *was* a prefab.

The inside of the portable was cold and lifeless and looked more like a funeral parlour than a classroom. An old-fashioned roller blind filtered the winter sun, shining a dead green light over the empty desks. There was only one picture on the wall: a washed out, glue-streaked poster advertising dental hygiene. The girl on the poster had freckles and a pigtail and the boy was wearing a brushcut. It could have sold as an antique at a flea-market. In comparison with the furniture in the main building, the desks and chairs of my portable looked like they had been scrounged from some storage warehouse for junked school furniture of the 1940s. Desks were hacked and gouged, while the wobbly chairs were often equipped with only three legs. The green blackboard was in such poor condition that you almost had to chisel letters onto it.

I can't recall many details from my first morning of actually working with my kids. Amidst the whirl, I tried to ignore their individual differences and treat them as one giant, uniform mass. I felt that if I lumped them into a single personality, I would be less overwhelmed.

Things went reasonably well during the first part of the morning (that is, if failing to remember most of what happened is synonymous with success). I was riding much too high to pay close attention to what I was doing. But when the first recess bell sounded, I received my inner-city initiation.

There was a concussive sound of glass breaking. Every window on the north side of my portable was smashed, simultaneously, in an instant! The rest of the day I remember well. I had to teach it in my woollen toque and Hudson's Bay blanket coat, while the kids murmured and laughed with nervous excitement, crouching next to the heat vents, which to their delight squeaked loudly. "Hey, this is neat!" one of the kids yelled.

The
Frontiers
of Despair

1

Monday, January 3

On my first day I made no attempt to disguise my gung-ho-I'm-gonna-wake-you-all-up-shake-you-up approach—I had my rookie determination.

I started my first session on "People and Society" by asking the kids what they wanted and expected from the course. Silence.

"Okay," I continued, undismayed, "let's try it this way. How many of you are interested in what goes on in the world today—the problems, the politics, the environment, the media, the job market—that sort of thing?"

Nothing. Blank eyes.

"Well," I went on, determined, with more than a small measure of arrogance, "I'm giving you kids the chance to choose the topic for yourselves. How about just a pinch more enthusiasm? What will it be?! Pollution? War? More rights for kids? How about some ideas for projects you want to do?"

No cheers. No boos. Not even a yawn.

I was almost shouting now in frustration. "What is it with you kids, anyway? If you can't think for yourselves, you might just as well quit school and join the army! Then you can take orders and never have to make a decision!"

Nothing.

Great, I thought to myself. *This is going nowhere.*

Maybe I'm expecting too much from these kids. Just when I thought everybody had been sworn to a conspiracy of silence, a kid wearing a Maple Leaf hockey sweater raised his hand. I felt like hugging him and called on him eagerly.

He asked: "Why do you wear a beard?"

Friday, January 7

I eagerly awaited the thrill of picking up my mail from my very own personal mailbox during my first trip to the office as an inner-city teacher.

Once inside the office, I saw a student lying on the bench. His knees were raised to his chest, arms holding them tight; he looked like a pale foetus. A second glance revealed a shiny piece of metal protruding from behind one of his ears. I looked closer. It was, in fact, a heavy steel dart lodged just above his ear.

Several kids had been playing darts outside when an argument broke out over whose turn it was. The boy responsible for throwing the dart was sitting in the vice-principal's office.

Apparently feeling no remorse, the kid merely sighed to a teacher who was watching. "He's just lucky I didn't hit him where I was aimin for!" I was waiting for a few abject tears, but there were none.

I stuck my head through the door to get a better view of the culprit. Sitting with his feet up on the vice-principal's desk, his face was split by an enormous yawn. Then: "Who are you, sucker? Are you the new teach? How'd you like a dart in your head? Hahaha . . . !"

Tuesday, January 11

The first day I was posted inside the main building on stair duty, they hit me in rapid-fire style from above. Ten or more kids spitting in unison. From the highest platform of the stairwell, the gobs of spit picked up quite an impact by the time they reached their mark—my head! And if I looked up to identify them, my face would offer an even more tempting target—it was disgusting enough having that scuzz through my hair.

When I chased up the stairs, I was too late. They had already disappeared into any of a dozen hiding places. Clearly, this situation called for strategy!

I gathered together some of the other teachers, and formed a plan. Some of us stood under stairwells at each recess, trying to inveigle the spit-kings to reappear, while other teachers crouched hidden, ready to rush out and grab the culprits.

We weren't able to catch them in the act. They were too smart. I gave up on strategy; today I began wearing a broad-rimmed hat during stair duty.

Friday, January 14

Levon arrived in the class this morning after recess—a transfer from another inner-city school.

Just before lunch, he was hit on the head by a flying book. I figured he could use a band-aid.

"Sanjay," I called out. "Will you please take Levon to the nurse's office?"

"Sanjay couldn't find his asshole with a roadmap," Duke interjected.

"I'll take him there," Winston volunteered.

"No! I will!" Spinner blurted out.

"Let me sir, please!" Taiwo insisted.

Before long, half the class marched out of the portable.

"It didn't need no band-aid," Levon said when he returned with the others after only fifteen minutes.

About two hours later, he complained of an upset stomach, and asked if somebody could show him to the nurse's office.

"But half the class took you there just a few hours ago," I reminded him. "Have you forgotten where it is already?"

"Oh, ya," Levon said with a wry smile on his lips. "That was only to show me the best place to grab a quick smoke."

Tuesday, January 18

One of the more colourful characters around the school is a twelve-year-old named Buddy. He's bold and he's black; one teacher compared him to railroad coal. Hated and feared—sometimes loved—Buddy literally runs the school, a role he plays with the virtuosity of an artist. He is a master technician when it comes to creating his own image. At a moment's notice he can become Lover, Fighter, Revenger, Champion of Freedom, King of the Sidewalks or Defender of the Dance. Everything and everyone is a point of reference for his act.

The kids in the school accord Buddy demi-god rank. When he walks down the corridor and says "Move over!" the kids move, fast! His voice is rarely loud, but it has a way of moving through the air like cold steel.

Even the teachers treat Buddy with a subtle deference. Any attempt at confrontation makes them nervous. He's only twelve, but he can immobilize you with a glance, quickening your breath, causing your heart to pound.

Why should we, grown men and women, be afraid of a kid, even if he is big for his age? Some of the teachers have no compunctions about treating kids roughly, if they have to. Yet this one kid could panic a whole school full of teachers. There are even warnings over the PA system when he's getting out of hand! He is ours, and for a variety of technical reasons, we keep him in school instead of tossing him out onto the unsuspecting world. We contain him, but we are all a little afraid of him. It may sound ridiculous that one kid should hold a group of adults in his grip . . . I'd find it hard to believe myself, if I didn't actually see it every day at the school. Well, what can we do? Beat up a twelve-year-old?

Buddy has an aggravating habit of fingering marbles, a bit like Captain Queeg in *The Caine Mutiny*. He rolls them unconsciously between his thumb and fingers like worry-beads, sometimes shaking them fiercely in a loosely clenched palm—a rattlesnake-like warning that he is about to strike. Those on his enemy list (which could include anybody) feel safe as long as the marbles are fingered in a relaxed sort of way.

Buddy is allowed to "float." Floaters roam the halls at will, as long as they don't leave the school building. To qualify as a floater, you have to be incorrigible, but in a soft, almost understated way. You have to conceal your violent behaviour, saving it up for strategic showdowns. Otherwise, the administration would send you away, to the "outside" or to another school.

Buddy spends most of the day wandering the halls with another floater named Puppy (because he's the youngest in his family). Buddy and Puppy spend their time window-shopping different classrooms for interesting things to do, always finding ways of breaking the monotony. They visit classrooms which have attractive girls, or they take karate lessons from the caretaker, or they smoke in the washroom.

Fred warned us that Buddy might appear unexpectedly in our classrooms. We were encouraged—coached—to respond in a highly positive way to any friendly gestures he might make. If you were lucky, Buddy would soon tire of you and float off somewhere else.

When you were teaching a class, it was unnerving to see Buddy pause at your doorway. He wore black boots, colourful dashikis, tight black cords. The flared bottoms of his pants had been lengthened three times. He was big and getting bigger. His Charles Atlas-like muscles made him a star attraction, and he seemed to walk an inch off the ground to the beat of an invisible disco tune. He was always in motion, always gesturing lewdly to Puppy. The first iron-clad rule when Buddy showed up was to appear to be in the middle of a boring lesson. The second rule: never turn on your record player—he tracked down music like a blood-hound—as long as there was music, he'd hang around, and if you tried to turn it off, you were in for trouble. Most of the staff avoided him.

When he wasn't floating, Buddy was in a special program for slow learners called a "developmental" class. Mr. Bailey, a jovial round-faced Welshman, ran it. Buddy's floating embarrassed him, and he decided to boost his reputation by trying to win Buddy back into the class for at least one day a week. Giving him more responsibility might be just the thing. Mr. Bailey decided to try leaving Buddy in charge of the class while he left to run off some stencils—a last ditch attempt by a desperate teacher to give Buddy a feeling of self-worth. It was a risky venture, and when Mr. Bailey returned the first thing he noticed was the blood on a kid's swollen lip. . . .

Once I thought that I could "vibe" Buddy away. Whenever I caught him standing outside my door, I would dilate my nostrils or curl my lips ever so slightly—just enough for him to pick up my hostility and go away.

But Buddy was a master of the unspoken. He said mouthfuls by using his eyes, or slowly licking his lips, or casually mopping his brow. His favourite gesture was to yawn loudly. Today, when I dilated and curled, he walked to the front of the room and picked his rear-end nonchalantly while the rest of the class howled. It was a humiliating experience.

He also tried running a protection racket. He would walk up to a kid in a corridor and say "Hey dude, how ya doin?" Then his lackeys would grab the kid from behind and drag him into the nearest washroom. Once inside, they would threaten to drastically rearrange the kid's face unless he brought them some money the next day. In the case of very little kids, Buddy insisted they bring him the funny green pieces of paper that mommy usually kept in her purse.

In a month or so, Buddy's empire confiscated well over a hundred dollars. By then the school administration discovered what was going on, and the police were called in to wrap up the racket.

"Where do you live?" one of the cops demanded of Buddy as they hauled him away. "We'll take you home."

Buddy smiled, then slowly pursed his lips. "Take me to Nova Scotia, man!"

Thursday, January 20

Ruth is exceptionally tall and good-looking, her skin sepia-coloured, her lips thick and sensuous. Her expression reminds me of a thin Elvis Presley. She's always raising her hand to be excused. When I asked her why she had to go to the bathroom so often, she told me it was due to "personal problems."

When I asked her if she had seen a doctor about the problem, she said no, it was a "women's problem," and to "mind my own bizness!" I replied that doctors knew all about "women's problems," that many doctors are women.

I sent her down to see the school nurse. It appeared that Ruth was pregnant.

Monday, January 24

Duke stands out in class. He wears black boots, tight pants and a shiny, red calypso shirt. Sometimes an old pork-pie hat is balanced precariously on his black mountain of hair. If he feels like it, he'll come into class wearing a woollen beret. Sometimes he tucks the beret into the epaulet of his safari jacket and salutes the flag in mock respect. He is, to put it mildly, a classic dude.

During the first week, Duke kept silent, sometimes cat-napping at his desk. Occasionally he'd shift his body around to check out the room.

Today I got fed up with his sleeping during a lesson I'd

worked particularly hard to prepare. I asked the kid next to him to wake Duke up. The kid touched him on the shoulder gingerly, as if he were disarming a bomb.

Suddenly Duke shot up from his chair, shouting: "Jesus! Don't do that, man, or I'll break your ass!" He was out the door in an instant.

I didn't see him until the end of the day. All he said was, "I fell asleep on the park bench."

Wednesday, January 26

From the beginning of the year it was obvious that Barry hero-worshipped Duke.

He admired his fighting ability—and was equally terrified of it. He toadied to Duke, fussing around him, running little errands for him.

His admiration shot up another notch as he watched Duke fight Sam. Duke hooked Sam with a left, then quickly decked him with a haymaker. Sam's mouth filled with blood, and he spit out bits of teeth.

Duke was a serious street-fighter, the star attraction for the school's would-be craftsmen in the pugilistic "art."

One day Duke turned on Barry. It was for no apparent reason, other than a lark—something to amuse Duke's other followers.

"The best way to teach you how to fight is to beat the shit out of you. Right?" Duke said, leering at Barry.

Barry cowered in terror. "Come on, Duke! Please!"

Duke walked closer to him.

"Stay back, Duke! Please! Just tell me what to do!" Barry pleaded in a plaintive, kid's whine.

Duke drew his arm back slowly, his fist clenched. He stood inches from Barry, ready to let fly.

"*I'll* do it for you, Duke! Here, *I'll* do it!" Barry screamed. Suddenly he grabbed his metal lunchbox, raised it over his head, then brought it down hard on his skull. There was a loud *crack*. He hit himself several times, until his lunchbox was hopelessly battered and blood trickled down his forehead.

"Okay, Duke? Okay?" Barry yelled.

Delirious and in tears, he found me in my classroom, and told me what happened.

Duke relished the fact that he didn't even throw a punch and still did all that damage.

"He did it all to himself, man," Duke said, gloating, when I questioned him. "He's some kind of nut."

Monday, January 31

Everybody called Francine "Muscle Lady." When she flexed her eleven-year-old's biceps, eyeballs popped. The boys were extremely jealous.

Muscle Lady wore a Superman tee-shirt to school with a plastic tiger's tooth hung from a piece of thread around her neck. And she always wore jeans with the legs turned up over her cowboy boots. When she walked by, you knew it was her by the sound of the clicking tacks she shoved into the heels of her boots.

Muscle Lady loved to fight—especially, boys. But boys didn't love to fight her. It was not only painful but humiliating when Muscle Lady had you pinned by the neck with her boot, and then bragged to the onlookers, "Should I cut off his balls?" If the crowd gave a "thumbs down" (which it usually did), Muscle Lady had been known to grind down her heel.

The word was out: If Muscle Lady has you in her sights, wear your steel hockey cup to school.

Tuesday, February 1

I was green. I wanted to change the world. Worse than that, I thought I could do it.

I obtained an 8mm. movie about World War Two from

a United Church clergyman. I had no idea where he got it, but I jumped at using it with my class.

The film was quite heavy. One section in particular, featuring Nazi war atrocities, would show my kids what war was all about! All I told them was that the film was about war, and that it was real footage—not actors playing roles.

As they watched the film, I watched their expressions. I waited expectantly for the sequence that showed Nazis carting dead bodies towards an open grave. I had no idea what the kids were thinking. Finally, the long unusual silence was shattered when a student cried out: "Stop the film!"

I thought to myself: My strategy worked after all! These kids now understand what war is all about!

I switched off the projector, ready to open up a discussion on the brutality of war. But the same voice in the darkness snapped: "Hey man. Turn the film backwards. Show that last part again. Did you see the arm falling off that dead body? Hahaha. That was cool! Let's see it again!"

Wednesday, February 2

It was the end of another school day. Duke, the tough dude, sauntered through the teachers' parking lot, sipping on a coke, and smoking. His after-school stroll often became the occasion for an impromptu gathering of his followers. Hordes of students trailed behind him, shouting "Hey, Duke!," or chanting his name: "Duke . . . Duke. . . ." Even teachers hailed him. His manner was always engaging, familiar: "Hiya pal. Whaddya say, baby?"

Everybody gathered around him, but always were careful not to crowd him.

"Hey, Duke!"

"Who ya punched out lately?"

"Hey Duke, whose pants ya been into this week?"

Today Duke was ordered off the school property for a few days: he had punched a kindergarten kid in the face, pushed him head-first into the fence, then stomped on his face.

His older sister was home when Fred phoned to explain that Duke could not return to the schoolyard. She promised she'd take care of him and keep him inside, but as soon as he walked through the door, she told him to get lost.

So he decided to wander down to the bicycle paths and torment some of the kindergarten kids there. Lots of them passed that way after school. He caught two boys who were running home and tripped them, pinching their ears. He tried to pull their pants down, taunting them in a whining voice: "Daddy's goin to give ya a beatin! Do what the daddy says! Be good little boys, and daddy won't beat ya no more!" When the children resisted, they were slammed to the ground. When Duke's mother returned home from work and heard what had happened, she waited for him with her hairbrush.

The next day, the parents of the injured kid reported Duke; the incident was investigated. He was suspended from school for a week, and his mother was given the name of a social agency she could contact.

When he returned to school, he was met as if he were an exiled king who had finally returned to lead his people into battle.

"Hey Duke baby!"

"Whaddya say!"

"Hey hey, the man is back!"

Friday, February 4

I was determined that I was going to open up these children to the world of knowledge, crack open those muffled minds. I was so convinced I would be able to turn their lives around; my career could do nothing but skyrocket over the next few years.

One Sunday afternoon my wife, Jenny, and I spotted a beautiful little home for sale in the Beaches, a fashionable part of Toronto that borders the lake. We decided we could afford it, and that evening our offer was accepted.

The contrast between our new neighbourhood and the Corridor was like day and night. Often, in the evening, we'd go for a brisk walk along the boardwalk by the lake; the sky and water helped soothe away some of the frustrations of the day.

Monday, February 7

Well, my teaching methods don't seem to be going over as well as I'd hoped; a lot of the kids are resistant to my lessons. I can't believe how defiant of authority these kids are—and they're only grades five and six! When I decided to swallow a little of my pride and ask for help, I went to see Fred.

"My lessons don't seem to be capturing the kids' attention," I told him, "even though they're right out of the latest books and programs available."

Fred laced his fingers behind his head, leaning back in his chair. "Peter, you know that even the most up-to-date textbooks are still only textbooks. Mostly our texts have middle-class settings that are irrelevant to our kids. Try some role-playing. It's a good technique with our kids. They like to act out situations. Ham it up, then see what you get."

The next day I proposed the idea to my class. Tina and Sandra volunteered at once to improvise a skit.

"What do you want to do it on?" I asked, noting happily how eager they seemed.

"Let's pretend I'm the husband," Tina suggested, "and this classroom is our apartment, and Sandra is my wife."

"Okay," Sandra agreed.

"I've just got home from work, and I find out you drank my case of beer. But you were supposed to do all the housework, see? Now you gotta explain why you didn't do no housework, and why you're drunk. Ready?"

As the rest of the class watched intently, Tina walked out of the room. She closed the door behind her, then knocked loudly. Sandra answered the door wearing a scowl on her face, pretending to be drunk. Tina stepped into the room, her arms held out in greeting.

"I'm home, honey," she called, trying to embrace Sandra (who resisted). "I'm so glad to come home to a clean house for a change!" She paused, looking around. "What are my clothes doing on the sofa? Your breath stinks of booze!" Tina pretended to shout, without really raising her voice. "Why are last night's dishes still piled in the sink? I oughta slap ya silly!"

"Why dontchya go to the track tonight?" Sandra mumbled, trying to slur her words. "Lemme alone. There's a good program on TV, and I don't wanna be disturbed."

"Disturb you! Why would I wanna do that?" quipped Tina. "Looks like nobody has disturbed you yet today! Why should I be different? Jus look at all those beer bottles on the floor! Get dressed and pick up this mess and fix me somethin to eat. Go on—move it!"

"Make it yourself!" Sandra snapped.

At this point, Tina was pretending to pick up the empty bottles and throw them away. "Just look at this place! It's a pig sty!"

With that remark, Sandra pretended to hit Tina on the head with a beer bottle. Tina responded by fighting right back, faking slaps at Sandra and screaming, "You good-for-nothin drunk! Why'd I marry you in the first place?!"

Thursday, February 10

Kids often show a bizarre sense of humour—they enjoy grossing out teachers with sick jokes and peculiar antics. I understood all that; I'd met lots of adults at parties who enjoyed doing exactly the same things. That's why I didn't think twice about Barry's jokes. I'd heard similar ones before.

For example, Barry would stroll into the classroom and ask me: "What do ya get when you take the wings off a fly?"

Before I could reply, he'd shoot back: "A walk, stupid! Hahaha!"

The first thing this morning, he asked me: "Hey, Mr. McLaren, what's green and goes 55 miles an hour?"

"I don't know, Barry. What?"

"A frog in a blender! Hahahaha! And waddya get when you add milk?" he asked.

"Beats me," I replied in an unconscious pun.

"A frog nog! Hahaha! Okay, last part. Whaddya do when you drink it?"

"Still stumped, Barry."

"You croak! Hahahaha!"

Or he once asked me: "What goes ha-ha clunk?"

"Don't know, Barry. What?"

"A man laughing his head off! Hahahaha!"

I almost started to appreciate Barry's sense of humour until a very reliable source informed me that, after school, Barry strangled cats.

Friday, February 11

Duke removed his winter coat and threw it on his desk. He was shirtless, dressed in dirty bib overalls. He slumped down in his chair, munching on a sandwich.

I was told at Teacher's College to lay down the rules on the very first day and stick to them.

"No eating in the room!" I commanded. "Put away the sandwich!"

Duke shut his eyes, nodded his head knowingly, and said softly (but not so softly that I couldn't hear), "It figures."

But he didn't leave it at that. "I ain't had no breakfast, so I'm just fillin up early on my lunch." He studied my reaction with cool disdain.

I looked at him angrily. He went on eating.

"What do you mean?" I asked, watching him uneasily, annoyed that he'd triggered off such a strong reaction in me. What was really bothering me was that I didn't know if he was putting me on or not. Maybe he *was* being sincere.

"Just gimme two seconds," he promised, his mouth crammed with salami. "There ... only one bite left," he mumbled, chewing hungrily. Then he smiled: "All gone! Now what was so bad about that?"

I closed my eyes, shook my head, indicating that I wasn't to be questioned further. There was an uneasy silence.

"Listen," I said, putting an end to the awkward moment. "It's all right."

He looked at me, then nodded impertinently. "Thanks, man. You can relax now, right?"

By the end of the day an eerie, engulfing sense of panic swept over me.

"What the hell are you doing here?" That was the question a voice in my head kept repeating over and over.

I crossed the parking lot quickly, anxious to get home. Several kids who were playing on the roof of my van jumped off as soon as I approached. For a few minutes I just sat inside, staring through the windshield at the steel-grey sky, the windswept grey high-rises towering in the distance. Everything seemed a mixture of white and black or in between—there wasn't a spot of colour in the entire landscape. I thought: the moon's surface probably has more charm than this.

When I reached home I was greeted by my nine-year-old step-daughter, Laura, her eyes blinking happily behind a pair of fluorescent cardboard glasses.

"How was school today?" I asked.

"Just great, dad!" she exclaimed. "Everybody got to make a pair of these glasses in art. The teacher bought all the material himself!"

I nodded, then asked her, "How do the kids in your class behave?"

"Everybody does what the teacher tells them to, prett well. Nobody even talks in class without the teacher's per mission."

"Nobody even talks," I echoed blankly. "I should be so lucky."

Laura groaned. "Gee, you're acting funny these days, dad."

Exhausted, I patted her on the head and made my way to the kitchen. My wife took one look at me, pursed her lips then sighed. "You look like—"

"Death warmed over, right?"

"Not even that good," she said. "Your eyes look glazed and your face is totally flushed."

That evening I fell asleep at the kitchen table. Laura claims she saved me from drowning in my soup. Somehow, Jenny managed to drag me to bed.

Monday, February 14

Teaching for a year in junior high-school in a wealthy neighbourhood had been a snap; disciplinary problems were few. My teaching style had been calm and friendly, and I rarely had reason to lose my temper. In a very short time, I realized that this school was another matter entirely. I would have to change my approach, since the kids either ignored me completely or else went to the other extreme, continually interrupting my lessons with wisecracks and smart-alec antics. Soon I was shouting, trying to get my lessons heard over the din. I threatened kids with after-school work or detentions if they didn't settle down.

But I found it hard to act "the heavy." The kids sensed my authoritarian image was merely a tactic, and called my bluff. When a class enjoys wearing down the patience of its teacher, all it needs is a hint that the teacher is out of control. Then it moves in for the kill.

Since my attempts at control were backfiring, I decided

to try another tactic. I did a John Wayne in *The Green Berets,* pacing in front of the class and barking orders:

"Sit up straight and tall!"

"Tuck in that shirt!"

"Eyes front!"

"Shape up or ship out!"

I didn't quite make it as the hard-boiled-drill-instructor-with-a-heart-of-mush, berating the kids into subservience on the theory that a good soldier obeys on reflex. That method got a few laughs, but not much else.

Sometimes I tried being *Barretta,* the tough TV detective: "Get those lessons done, kids, on accounta they're an important part of growin up!"

"Keep on strokin!"

"Reading will keep you off the streets, outta trouble, and outta the slammer!"

The kids thought I was a weirdo.

Tuesday, February 15

After the kids returned from gym, I asked them what improvements they'd like to see me make in the classroom.

"You ain't gonna leave the room like that bitch had it?" Duke asked, cocking his head to one side.

"What was wrong with the room?"

"We didn't like the set-up!" he barked back. "We didn't like havin no spare time! It was always work, man!"

Levon stood up and walked to the back of the room, with a ruler stuck out of his open fly. "We wanna teacher with big boobs!"

Marianne, one of my West Indian girls, rose out of her chair. "We wants a black teacher!"

"A black teacher with big boobs!" Levon cut in.

"Naa!" someone else cried. "Who wants a fuzz-top for a teacher?"

"When are we gonna play floor hockey?"

"What about field trips?"

"Can we play records in class?"

For the rest of the day, I was swamped with questions. For me, the questions themselves were part of the solution. The kids were coming out of their shells, testing me out, airing some of their frustrations.

Any reasonable suggestion, I made a note of, and tried to do something about.

It was too early to know what they made of me, but I was confident that if they would only give me a chance, they would grow to like me. I wanted that chance badly.

Wednesday, February 16

Duke and Al paired off cautiously. From an upper window, I saw what looked like the entire school population in the main yard, surrounding the two fighters. The crowd was cheery and talkative, in gleeful anticipation of the bout. Students jerked, twisted, strained to see the fight. I started at once for the stairs.

The shouting got louder and louder, the excitement feeding on itself, swelling with hoots and whistles.

"Kill him!"

"Break the sonofabitch's balls!"

"Punch his eyes out!"

I heard fever-pitch wails as I burst through the main door. Drops of bright red blood spattered the pavement.

Duke's foot shot out in a blur. Al coughed and gagged, finally dropping to his knees. "Ya goddam motherfucker!"

Smooth as a cobra, Duke took another short step forward. "Fuckin nigger bastard!" A lightning kick to the solar plexus. The kids were screaming for blood ... my commands to stop were lost in the roar.

This time Al fell on his side, screaming in pain. A hard kick in the ribs as he tried to raise himself up. Another. Four swift kicks to the head. Al's eyes rolled up. To break up the fight, I had to fight my way through the eager crowd.

Thursday, February 17

I don't like looking out the windows of my portable. The view is too bleak: an inner ring of identical little bungalows, with an outer perimeter of ugly high-rises. The small park near the school is only a partial buffer against the impersonal, almost anonymous, surroundings.

During role call, I realized that over half my kids had the same address—a large government-subsidized building nicknamed "The Jungle" by some teachers. Only one kid lived in a "regular" house, and only a few lived in the public complex of townhouses.

When I asked my kids what they did with their free time, they answered:

"Play in the laundromat until the super kicks us out."

"Go to the arcade at Food City."

"Ride the elevator."

"Me and Buddy," Levon offered eagerly, "watch the teenagers screw each other in the basement!"

As Fred once mentioned to me, "The only thing worse than being poor is being poor in the suburbs."

Friday, February 18

Nearby is a Catholic school that the kids nicknamed St. Welfare. One morning last week, Levon crawled through a hole in the fence and crept up to a window. He watched the students going through the morning's opening exercises, and when he finally showed up in *my* class, he described them in vivid detail.

"The whole class started to pray all at once to this cross on the wall. But there were some guys at the back of the room who were playin with hockey cards—the teacher didn't see em cause her eyes was closed. Hey, sir. Why don't them Catholic teachers pray with their eyes open?" He grinned, and scratched his head. "Anyway, sir, how come them Catholic kids get to talk to God, and we don't?"

Levon's last remark caught me a bit off guard. I quietly retreated to my desk, stalling for time.

"Well . . ." I hesitated, "we don't say prayers in class because this is a public school, and kids come here belonging to different religions. Some people believe in different Gods, and some people don't believe in God at all."

Levon looked puzzled, but he shrugged. "Who cares about talkin to God, anyway? I heard this story from a lady in my buildin that God was born in a barn, with a bunch of cows and donkeys, and she says He slept on some straw on the floor. Is God really on welfare?"

Monday, February 21

When I was teaching junior-high, I had set foot in the principal's office only once. I had been put on the carpet because I had allowed some of my students to call me by my first name.

Fred's office, on the other hand, was a place where I spent considerably more time—but for different reasons. Fred kept his office open so teachers could use it whenever it was free.

Because Fred did most of his paperwork in the staff-room, teachers could use his office for phone calls, or to help themselves to the stacks of educational books and journals he stashed in a big box in the corner marked "Free." He had also replaced the standard-issue grey desk with a pine coffee table, as well as replacing his chrome and vinyl chair with a Boston rocker. One wall of his office was totally devoted to the kids' art.

Often, teachers went to his office simply to relax.

The vice-principal's office was right next door. Rod had the same open-door policy, but he spent more time in his office, so it wasn't as available to the teachers.

Today when I stepped inside Rod's office to use the phone, I found him sitting in his chair, calmly holding a struggling black kid.

"Would you mind watching this guy for me while I go get a coffee? I'm bushed."

"Sure, Rod."

"He went beserk in Mrs. Rogers' room. Just make sure he doesn't get out the door."

After Rod left, the kid simply smiled and quietly sat down in a chair in the corner of the office. I sat down in Rod's chair, picked up a magazine, and started skimming pages, the phone call temporarily delayed.

Suddenly, I was knocked right out of my chair by a blow from behind. I looked up from the floor to see the kid standing over me with a hockey stick!

I got to my knees, propping myself up on the arm of the chair, but before I made it to my feet the kid yanked the chair away, and I fell back on the floor.

"Vanilla trash!" the kid snarled, and ran out the door.

Rod came back into his office a few minutes later to find me alone, tucking my shirt in and rubbing my sore, throbbing neck.

"Let me guess," Rod said. "You let him escape."

Tuesday, February 22

Each day the build-up in my mailbox grew. Curriculum materials, surveys, advertisements for curriculum materials, and surveys to establish an advertising policy. Subject guidelines, policy guidelines, guidelines for guidelines—it seemed endless.

At first, in my naivete, I figured everything was important and actually read it all. Somehow the educational system was nourished by all these forms and papers. However, I soon realized that I'd receive something worthwhile maybe once a week. Teachers, I learned, referred to mailbox build-up as "Administrivia."

One day, feeling particularly grumpy, I simply picked up the latest pile of papers and dumped them all into the garbage.

"Hey!" a seasoned veteran exclaimed. "You'd make a great principal!"

Thursday, February 24

In spite of the fact that Ricky got on my nerves, I wouldn't call his parents for help when he got into trouble.

It was too possible that what Ricky said was true . . . that when his parents heard he had done something wrong, they strapped him on top of the dining room table and, taking turns with a belt, beat him.

Friday, February 25

Kids called Marianne "Big Mama."

She was a giant of a girl with the most beautiful braids of any West Indian child I had ever seen. The top of her head looked like a black patch-work quilt with white stitching. Her mother had given her a button which she wore proudly. It read: "Kid for Rent (cheap)."

She became a legend one day by giving Duke an unprecedented defeat. She simply knocked him off his feet with a swoop of her huge hand, and then sat on his chest until he almost turned blue.

There was little sexual stereotyping in my class.

Saturday, February 26

Jenny and I were driving through the Jane-Finch area, so we decided to do some shopping at the local plaza.

Inside the crowded mall were people of every size, shape and colour. Packed into the Miracle Mart, Food City and Dominion stores were Italian mothers in black kerchiefs, West Indian families in matching dashikis, teenagers dashing madcap through the aisles and scores of young kids at the pinball machines.

One of the most popular stores catered to tee-shirt lovers. Anything could be printed on a tee-shirt while you waited. My wife got in line. She turned up later with a tee-shirt with "Super Teach" printed on it.

As we were going out I spotted four of my students hanging out in the parking lot. Duke and Jackson were wobbling and slurring their words. Dave was sneezing violently, and Lisa was laughing, hiding her face. Duke had a smaller, frightened kid backed into a corner, cold-bloodedly trying to provoke a fight. They all looked very high on something.

"Is this what you kids do on weekends?" I asked, giving the frightened kid a chance to run away.

"We're not *kids* on the weekend," Jackson said. "On the weekend, we're the Dukes!"

Tuesday, March 1

The teachers were all crowded around a notice posted on the staff bulletin board. It was the new yard duty schedule, still smelling from duplicating fluid. Because I had been hired in mid-year, my name hadn't appeared on the first list. That oversight had now, unfortunately, been corrected.

Yard duty meant the entire school population at once—over six hundred kids crowded together at recess in a mass of swirling bodies.

Near the main entrance, a group of kids huddled under a blanket, trying to walk together. They only managed to make this giant insect move a few feet at a time before they tripped all over each other's legs. Across the yard, a group of kids stood around the drinking fountain. A tiny kindergarten kid was pushed against the metal water faucet. "He's kissin Farah Fawcett!" one of them cried.

I ran across the yard, but was too late. I had two girls from my class take the kid to the office to have his bleeding gums looked after. Meanwhile, kids played marbles or made bets on which way baseball cards flung against the wall would land.

A kid with a frantic look led me to the other side of the yard where I found a little six-year-old girl tied to the fence. She was being swatted across the legs by an older boy armed with a tree branch. When I grabbed the boy, he sneered defiantly, "Whatta ya doin! Eh? She's my sister, ya know! I can do what the fuck I like with her!" and then he took off like a rocket. I untied her, and my two little Florence Nightingales led her inside the school.

When the bell sounded, I thanked God.

Thursday, March 3

Jenny has begun to worry about me. When I return home from work I usually go directly into the den and close the door. I prefer not to talk to anyone and just sit there doodling on a piece of paper. I half-started working on a series of children's stories that were about the real world as opposed to the world of magic and make-believe, but after about an hour that depressed me, too. My one real outlet is playing my guitar. I've taught myself how to use a bottleneck and try to imitate some of the Delta blues artists who played out of the Mississippi region in the early 1920s. It gives me a tremendous emotional release.

"Play something cheery for a change!" Jenny complains.

Monday, March 7

After a few weeks of trying to teach my kids according to the Ministry guidelines and the approaches I had been taught in my teacher training, I knew that I would either have to change my entire approach or sacrifice my stomach. My health had been suffering. I continually caught colds, had dizzy spells, stomach cramps. Sometimes I threw up in the staff washroom after a hard day.

I thought I wanted to learn more about what makes kids hate so much, so I decided to enroll in a Master's program in education, even if it was only part-time. For two evenings a week I would study the sociology of the poor, as well as child management.

Fred was glad that I showed concern, but he disagreed with my strategy: "You *already* know these kids are poor," he told me patiently. "You *already* know most of them come from single-parent families, and you *already* know that a great majority of them are beaten up at home. So what's a university course going to teach you?"

I stared at the ceiling. I knew the point he was making, but I finally said I'd still like to try it.

"If it makes you feel better, Peter, you have my blessings."

Wednesday, March 9

I was anxious to get some feed-back from the rest of the staff, and I looked forward to our lunchtime conversations in the staff room.

The room itself was starting to look quite attractive. Some of the teachers were redecorating it, trying to achieve a coffee-house atmosphere. Hieronymous Bosch prints hung on all the walls, and the shell of an old radio was placed over the intercom speaker. The librarian fitted the tables with plastic checkered tablecloths, and volunteers (kids included) brought in empty wine bottles to hold candles. One teacher described it as "creating a buffer."

This afternoon I took a seat beside a teacher I hadn't seen before. She introduced herself as a supply teacher who had been working the area for a while. I was struck by how much she looked the caricature of the spinster teacher: hair in a bun, horn-rimmed glasses, worn tweed jacket. Even though she wore plenty of make-up, she still reminded me of the middle-aged ladies I saw in church when I was a child. "How do you like being an inner-city teacher?" she asked.

"Things are getting easier," I replied. "I'm doing a lot of reading . . . trying to discover some tricks for coping. By the way, what kind of techniques do *you* use with the kids? Maybe we can exchange ideas."

She cleared her throat, looking down at her lunch, smiling. "There *is* one thing that I find helps me make it through the day," she said softly.

"Yes?"

"I never talk about the kids during lunch. That's *my* secret for success!"

Thursday, March 10

Jabeka had a pile of letters on her desk that her mother asked her to mail, three of which were addressed to relatives in Spanish Town, Jamaica.

"Have you been back to visit since you've come to Canada?" I asked her.

"Are you kiddin, Mr. McLaren?" she replied. "My father is in Jamaica and no way do I wants to see him. My mother don't wants to see him, no way. Ever since we come to Canada, my dad don't bother callin us. He never writes no letters, or calls collect on the phone—not even Christmas."

"How long have you been away from your father?"

"Five years. Ever since we come to Canada. I gots a step-dad now. He's gots two kids who live with his other wife right next to Food City. His wife's gots a boyfriend named Mr. Jimmy who's gots three kids. Mr. Jimmy buy all the best food for his own kids."

"What does your real father do in Jamaica?" I asked, trying to maintain a casual tone.

"He lives with his girlfriend. I gots two other brothers there but they don't live with my dad. They lives with my grandmother—you know, my dad's mother."

"So you never see your other brothers?"

"Last time I was in Jamaica, and then me and my mother moved away. I went to visit my grandmother and she told me to go back to where I belong."

"Where was that, Jabeka?"

"How the hell is I supposed to know? With my mother, I guess!"

"So your parents split up before you came to Canada?"

"Yah! I still wants to visit my dad sometimes. He likes me more than his girlfriend because when we was comin back from shoppin there he told his girlfriend to get off his motorcycle and he puts me on the back."

"Do you have any other brothers and sisters living with you?"

"I gots a younger brother and a younger sister. I don't know if they come from my real dad, but my mom says they're my brothers. My step-dad and my mom just made a baby, but it's not born yet."

"Are you glad you came to Canada, Jabeka?"

"Yah," she replied. "We never had no coloured TV in Spanish Town."

Monday, March 14

During recess, Spinner and Duke, opponents in ball hockey, started to argue over whether or not to allow a last-minute goal. Duke decided to settle the issue his way: he punched Spinner in the mouth. Spinner reeled backwards, knees buckling. Duke kicked him in the groin as he fell.

His moans were heard by the teacher on yard duty, and he was taken to the hospital with a bleeding penis.

Spinner's mother showed up at the school later that afternoon. "Show me Duke!" she demanded.

A tiny kid wearing a mass of dreadlocks said, "There!," and pointed to the open gym doors. Spinner's mother spied Duke, and after taking a huge drag on her cigarette, suddenly bolted down the corridor after him.

I ran to stop her.

She caught up to Duke in time to drag him to the floor and punch him. I managed to get between them. Then I calmed Spinner's mom down. Duke hadn't been injured.

"He got what was coming to him!" she told me triumphantly, smacking her lips with satisfaction.

Rod took Spinner's mother into the office, and I turned to Duke. "How're you feeling?" I asked him.

"Okay," Duke said, panting. "Okay. Nothin's busted. Shee-it! What a suck that Spinner is—sendin his momma over to take care of his own bizness."

Tuesday, March 15

An announcement came over the PA system regarding a potluck luncheon for the teachers.

"Potluck, eh?" Ricky mused. "What's you bringin, sir?"

"Pot or hash?" Duke called out.

"My brother's got some dynamite Colombian at home! You want some?" Spinner volunteered.

Wednesday, March 16

The lunch bell sounded.

Children exploded from the doors and poured in to the halls. Unresolved arguments that had accumulated during the morning were now settled with fists. The air was thick with screams, shouts and well-chosen obscenities. A contingent of teachers and lunchroom supervisors waded through tiny human walls, challenging kids who refused to leave the halls. "I gotta wait for my mom!" "My teacher said I don't gots to leave!" "I gotta wait for my little sister!" The excuses sounded convincing.

Kids screamed louder and louder while balls, paper airplanes, and plastic hockey pucks flew through the air.

A teacher with hair swarming all over her head, and her kids still swarming all over her classroom, ran out the door in tears. "Damn these kids! I can't take it!"

Mothers met their children in the halls to conduct them safely home. From the schoolyard could be heard do-wah medleys in sweet, piercing falsettos.

Finally weary, overtaxed teachers retreated to the staff room and quickly shut the door behind them.

Thursday, March 17

Buddy tore madly around the yard, pummelling everyone he passed on the back with a windmill series of quick blows. When the terrified kids fled, he stood in the middle of the empty corridor and threw Muhammad Ali jabs at his shadow. He was celebrating his new, red boxing gloves—initiating them, breaking them in. For Buddy, all the world was a ring.

It was my duty to tell him that gloves were not allowed in school. I figured he'd tell me where to get off. What he casually said was, "If you want me to stop, you gotta go me a few rounds first. I'll bring my brother's pair this afternoon."

Great.

At the end of the day, kids of all ages poured into my room. Buddy was one of the last to enter. I figured it wouldn't be too bad. After all, I stood six feet and weighed 165 pounds. Buddy was a twelve-year-old kid, even if he was big for his age.

Applause accompanied his entrance. Even members of my own class cheered him; they had just as much a right to their own protection after school as anybody else.

Buddy began wrenching his neck back and forth in an impressive limbering-up ritual. We tied on our gloves; everyone waited in suspense.

Suddenly he rushed me, almost bowling me over. I gave him one light jab to keep him back. Then I stood ready, and we began to box.

"You can do betteran that, McLaren!"

"Come on, Buddy—move it!"

"Hitem in the nuts!"

"You're okay, man!"

After the first few rounds I was tiring noticeably, while Buddy grew stronger and more confident. I wasn't trying to land solid punches, but Buddy was determined to knock me out. In about three years, he would be able to kill me!

I finally ended the match gracefully by saying I had to leave and get to a course. Buddy stood perspiring, in a classic boxing stance. He accepted my decision to stop the fight and walked over. "You put on a pretty good show, man," he said, not too confidentially, so everyone would hear. "Of course, I coulda decked you anytime, but I don't want you to look like a dummy in front of the kids."

Friday, March 18

In Teacher's College, budding young professionals were guaranteed at least one "sure-fire" lesson. It would always work, no matter who the kids or what the class. In moments of desperation this lesson could turn a would-be disaster into a fantastic success. Or so the theory went.

In a moment of panic, I decided to haul out my "sure-fire" lesson. I wrote two sentences on a piece of paper—an opening and a closing sentence. The kids had to fill in the story by contributing one sentence, then passing the paper to the next kid.

My opening sentence was: "I wish I had more friends like the ones I met last summer." The closing sentence: "It was the most exciting vacation I ever had."

It seemed to be working. The kids were getting into it and the class quieted down, with a few giggles and knee-slapping.

The finished product read:

"I wish I had more friends like the ones I met last summer. I met a girl in a bikini. She had big tits. Don't write so dirty, Duke. Shut up Tina, and let him write what he feels like. I put my hands on her big knockers and squeezed them. We necked a lot. She felt my giant cock. Change the subject. Then we went into my cottage. . . ."

Monday, March 28

Let's have art this afternoon, Mr. McLaren!
Yah. We want art!

Well, we've got some math to do this afternoon. Perhaps after we're finished with that . . .

We wanna naked model . . . one with really big tits that stick out to here!

. . . and lots of fuzzy hair down here!

You guys are sick! Is that all you think about?

Shut up Sandra! All you think about is naked boys!

Barry's a fag. He thinks about naked boys, too!

Fuck you, you stupid morons!

Let's keep the language clean, okay? Can we drop this naked model business and get on with the math lesson!

Wash out your mouth, Barry! You said fuck about a hundred times today!

Fuck off!

A hundred and one.

Hey sir, Barry's got the tail of a cat tied to the aerial of his bike!

It's a racoon's tail! I bought it at the store!

Sir! Let's have floor hockey instead!

I hates floor hockey!

We don't want you girls! Hey, sir! Let the girls play skippin or somethin, but let us play floor hockey!

There will be no playing anything until we finish our math!

Kids should be allowed to choose sometimes. You said so!

Yah! You never let us have fun—real fun!

Okay, okay. What does "real fun" mean?

If we wanna go somewheres, the creek or somethin, then you should let us . . .

Duke just wants to finger Sandra!

You're dead! After school you're gonna get two black eyes and you're gonna swallow your teeth, you smartass!

Hold it, Duke! Settle down, okay? Open your books to the math review on page fifty-one.

Wait a minute! I ain't gots no pencil!

That's because you used it to jab that little kid at recess

and the teacher took it off you!

Get lost . . .

Here, you can use my pencil.

Thanks, sir! Hey look! I stole the teacher's pencil!

Can I turn on the radio during art?

Quietly yes . . . quietly. But first, our math!

Hey Sandra, get up on the desk and take off your shirt!

Shaddup! Why don't you get up there and whip out your prick?

Question number one! You've got three minutes!

Hey, I need to go to the bathroom! Stop the test! If I don't go now, I'm gonna shit my pants!

Let's draw his shit!

Yah, I wanna draw his turds!

Anybody who doesn't finish this test gets a note to take home and get signed!

Sir! Can I have a note, please! I love notes!

Me too! I wanna note sayin I'm bad!

Everybody line up for bad notes!

Hurry up Levon! Whip down those pants and shit on your desk! I wanna draw your stinky plops.

Hey! Gimmie back my math book!

Cut out the crap!

This is boring . . .

Tuesday, March 29

Levon's father stumbled through the door and took a chair. He wore a faded blue tee-shirt which had "Unemployed With Dignity" stencilled across the chest. After checking out the room, he asked me where the washroom was.

"The boys' john is around the corner," I said.

On his way out, he turned and said, "Ya don't really buy beer, ya know. Ya rent it."

On his return, I showed him a short story his son had written a week earlier. It began:

It was so nice out, I decided to leave it out all day. I didn't feel like going to school, so I stayed home and watched the Flintstones on TV.

It ended:

Life is like a prick. When it's hard you get fucked. When it's soft you can't beat it.

Levon's dad looked at me and smiled. "Takes right after his old man, don't he?"

Wednesday, March 30

I asked the kids to act out what they saw daily on television.

Vince did a beautiful number on the Sunday evangelical TV shows by having the host of the program repeat the words "Praise the Lord!" while he made a move on one of his voluptuous guests.

Frank and Sanjay did a put-on of two cops busting a group of dissident youths for smoking pot. Then the two cops took it home for themselves.

Hamlin, a frustrated kid, made up a character he called Super Student, who went through the school socking malefactors and bumbling, bigoted, short-sighted teachers.

But in my opinion, the best was Tina's portrayal of a movie starlet. She emerged clad in a scintillating red smock, with a matching hat and scarf. She tossed aside her hat, unwound her scarf and dropped her smock to reveal two enormous breasts. The huge globes resulted from the strategic insertion of two soccer balls under her sweater.

Tina also had another ball thrust up her back, which she described as her "spare boob—it'll start a new trend in Hollywood!"

Thursday, March 31

There was a loud knock at the door. Spinner answered it, and was almost bowled over by Mark's mother as she stormed up to my desk.

"Gimme Mark!" she demanded.

Mark slumped down in his seat, peering timidly over the edge of his desk.

"Mark," I said, "you'd better go with your mother."

No sooner had Mark walked to the front of the room than his mother had him pinned to the blackboard.

"Who was it, Mark?!" she ordered.

"I don't know! Lemme go!" Mark pleaded.

"Not until you tell me the name of the kid that beat you up and took my twenty dollars! You stupid jerk! Why'd ya tell him you had twenty bucks on you for?"

"I don't know!" Mark whined.

By now the whole class was quietly watching. Dave, another West Indian kid, asked: "Was he black?"

"No, he was goddam honkey white," Mark answered, head down.

"You goddam well pick him out of some class! Mr. McLaren, I'm taking Mark for a walk aroun the school!" She half-dragged him out of the room.

Mark found the kid in a grade six class. He still had ten dollars in his pocket. Mark's mom took the kid by the scruff of the neck, and hauled him to Fred's office.

Later, she returned Mark to class.

"I don't know what you're gonna do with this one," she said. "Sometimes he can get so stupid, he don't know whether to fart or turn blue!"

Monday, April 4

Burt always seemed to know what was troubling me, even though I tried to keep my problems to myself.

He could tell if I didn't get enough sleep the night before, whether or not I was feeling rotten, or if I wasn't getting along with a particular staff member that day. Burt seemed to possess some special capacity for reading people's minds . . . or else he was one damn good guesser!

For example, today Burt blurted out: "Hey kids! Mr. McLaren's in a good mood today! That's cause Spinner hasn't shown up yet! Mr. McLaren can't stand the way Spinner snaps his gum when he chews. Right, Mr. McLaren?" He grinned. And continued. "You hate Spinner's buck teeth, too—dontchya, Mr. McLaren? You think they make him look like a donkey! Am I right? I'm right, ain't I, sir?" He refused to stop. "Mr. McLaren's probably prayin right now that Spinner's sick, and not just late for class. Hey, Mr. McLaren! You got both fingers crossed?"

They were.

Thursday, April 7

Faisel's mother spoke Arabic—but no English. When she was called into the school to settle an argument between Faisel and Mrs. Rogers, Faisel did the translating.

Mrs. Rogers had caught Faisel walking out of the school with some expensive gym equipment. He claimed he had found it, and was merely checking to see if there was a teacher in the yard he could return it to.

Faisel's mother stormed into the foyer of the school, her arms waving and her fists clenched. She started screaming at Mrs. Rogers in Arabic.

"What's your mother saying?" Mrs. Rogers asked.

"She says that this is a nice school, this is a wonderful country, you are a nice lady, and I would never steal a thing," Faisel replied, with an ingratiating smile on his lips.

Faisel's mother began shaking her fist in the air.

"What's she saying now?"

"She says not to be mad at me because I am a nice, polite boy and come from a good home," Faisel interpreted.

Faisel's mother looked frustrated. She lifted up her blouse and showed Mrs. Rogers a large bandage over her belly.

"Come on now, Faisel," Mrs. Rogers demanded. "What has your mother really been saying?"

"Okay," Faisel said. "I'll tell you. She's swearing at you cause she just got out of the hospital and you made her get out of bed to come down here!"

Tuesday, April 12

After school, over a cigarette and coffee, Fred filled me in on a bit of his background.

He had been hired here as principal after serving four years in another inner-city school in the west end. It was there that his reputation as the "hugging principal" grew. Articles were written about him, and he was invited on several TV talk shows to speak about his philosophy of reaching kids through improving their self-concept.

The main reason he had put so much effort into his previous school was because his wife had died prior to the appointment, and in a very real sense he had become married to the school.

Teachers were so devoted to Fred's method that they involved themselves in group therapy sessions, and often stayed until eight or nine in the evening working out new programs for the kids. "Several marriages suffered badly," he told me. "Teachers seldom made it home to see their spouses before bedtime."

When the former principal retired, the staff had decided they wanted a definite say in who would be chosen to succeed him. They formed a committee and approached the Board, offering a list of qualities the new principal should possess. After all, a school in the Jane-Finch Corridor had special needs, and a special person was needed to help fill them as principal.

When the staff heard that Fred was available, they called a staff meeting to decide if he would be suitable. Except for a few teachers who preferred a more authoritarian type, the majority agreed they liked Fred's philosophy.

He was hired in September, four months before he hired me.

"At our first staff meeting," he told me, "the teachers told me they wanted me to do here what I had done at my former school. I told them about my wife dying, and that was one of the reasons I had put everything I had into my work. I also explained that since that time I had remarried, and my wife was expecting a baby soon. I knew I wouldn't be able to give as much as I had previously, but I promised I'd do my best to bring a better program into the school."

Thursday, April 14

During art, Donnie drew a picture of Sharon squeezing her breasts and squirting great jets of milk into the air, and then left the drawing on Sharon's desk, waiting for her reaction.

She reddened, gritting her teeth. Crouching low, she charged and split open Donnie's cheek with a head-butt. Her eyes widened when she saw the sight of blood.

Donnie stemmed the flow with his shirt tail and retreated to his desk. I sent him down to the nurse.

"Stupid prick!" Sharon hollered. "The dummy don't even know ya gotta be pregnant before you squirt milk!"

Friday, April 15

After teaching in the area for a few months, I was aware of what the environment could do to the kids. Every so often I would see new kids with impeccable records turn into sad, battered little things. It was the particularly meek and timid child that drew my sympathy.

Such a child was Krishna, a miniature bespectacled Mahatma Gandhi. On his second day he walked timidly up to my desk. "Sir, some girls in the other class beat me up after school."

I knew he would have a tough time.

But Krishna got the break he deserved. His father bought him a motorcycle tee-shirt, black polyetheline boots, and a leatherette jacket with lots of zippers and studs. It's a very effective disguise.

Monday, April 18

Before I started teaching, I assumed any hyperactive kids would be in special classes; I had no idea there would be so many in my "ordinary" classroom.

John, a fellow teacher, told me that kids in the area were particularly undernourished, and that could not be disputed. He thought the kids probably were suffering from allergic reactions to the food dyes in all the junk food they ate. He also told me that the fluorescent lights installed in every classroom affected behaviour, making kids jumpy, making them lose control. "Shut off those lights! Keep your blinds wide open!" he advised, looking up from his latest copy of *Prevention* magazine.

I found the bit about fluorescent lighting eccentric, to say the least, but I was desperate enough to try anything. I usually kept my venetian blinds angled downwards, to shut out the view—the slightest thing would distract the class.

Today I threw caution to the winds and opened them as far as I could. From the open windows long shafts of honey-coloured sunlight fell across the kids' faces, highlighting the faint cloud of chalk dust, bathing the room in a golden haze. The kids' faces appeared almost angelic.

After about ten minutes of peace, Duke decided to go on "scrap patrol," dragging the wastepaper basket around the room, collecting all the paper that had fallen on the floor. Then, like a bulldozer out of control, he crashed his way through a row of desks, elbowing the kids along the way. Sally tried to avoid him, only to fall backwards in her chair. Then Robbie and Sharon, ignoring all the commotion, sauntered up to the blackboard, each trying to outdo the other in a graffiti competition.

Clutching at their groins, Levon and Frank asked me if they could be excused. They ran out, giggling, to the main building, not bothering to wait for an answer.

Duke must have noticed the grimace on my face, because he bounded up to my desk with a puzzled look on his face. "Hey, sir, . . . what's with you?"

I gave natural light a chance for the next few hours, but then the kids began throwing things out the open windows.

One of the teachers was delighted to bring this to Fred's attention. He suggested it would be a good idea to keep my blinds closed in the future—natural light notwithstanding.

Friday, April 22

At my previous school, I remember the boasts of the staff I overheard during lunchtime:

"One girl in my grade eight class is already working on advanced calculus!"

"One of mine already has a firm grasp of quantum physics!"

"I have a student who will be the next Emily Carr!"

Whereas the bragging of inner-city teachers was of a different nature:

"Three kids in my class have been to court this year for vandalism!"

"One of my girls was so hard to handle it took three of us, including Fred!"

"Two of my students shot at each other with .22s from the balconies of their apartments, and say they'll shoot me if I hassle them!"

They often painted the most dismal picture possible of their students, competing over who had the toughest kids, the worst problems; it was their red badge of courage.

Monday, April 25

Rod asked me if I'd mind taking over the lunch-hour duty; the regular supervisor was off sick. "You're pretty good with the kids," he said. With that remark, I was able to chalk up my first real compliment of the year. He explained that the kids were given half an hour to eat, and then were led, by me, outside to be supervised during play in the schoolyard.

The kids were already eating when I arrived. The place was in an uproar; food was spread all over the place, if you could call some of it food: pop, twinkies, chocolate pudding, oreo cream wafers, brownies, hot dogs, peach pits, salami rinds, bread crumbs, potato chips, cheesies, etc. etc. etc.

I took my place at the supervisor's desk, watching quietly. There was as much food-trading going on as food-eating. Right away one kid tried to trade me his bologna sandwich for my ham-on-a-kaiser, saying his cost twice as much.

Every so often I ducked flying baseball cards. Music mysteriously blared from a car parked across the street, the kids tapping their feet to it. And I swear every kid took his empty lunch bag, blew it up and exploded it with a bang!

A little black boy wearing a sea-island shirt and wire-framed sunglasses stood up and danced "the robot" for a group of clapping girls, his dreadlocks flapping.

At the half-hour mark, I told the kids it was time to go outside. Sandwich wrappings flew everywhere in the delicate stampede out the door.

Once outside, I breathed a sigh of relief—that is, until I heard screams coming from the sand pit. A big red-headed kid had tied a piece of glass to the end of a broken hockey stick and was gleefully charging a terrified pack of fleeing behinds. He held a garbage-pail lid as a shield, and wore an inverted plastic funnel as a helmet. I took the weapon from this miniature Don Quixote, which he didn't like at all.

"Gimmie back my spear, you son-of-a-bitch!"

"Sorry, weapons aren't allowed on school property," I said crisply.

"Hand it over or I'll break your ass, man!"

I pried the glass off the end of the stick, and threw it over the fence.

"You're new here," the kid drawled, "ain't ya, turkey?"

That afternoon, as I was pulling out of the school parking lot, I glanced down at the dashboard. The eight-track stereo I kept locked in my car was missing.

Wednesday, April 27
Duke and his mom and dad had moved down to the Jane-Finch area from a mining community in northern Ontario. The only work the father managed to find lasted merely six weeks. Soon after, he packed it in and headed back up north; Duke and his mother stayed behind.

"No way I'm heading back up north," she told me today during an interview, a tremor of irritation in her voice. "There's nothing up there. The city is where you make it. Everybody knows that. I'm looking for a job as a key-punch operator. If I can get that, well it won't be easy street, but maybe we'll finally move out of this dump. I don't like the gang that Duke's been hanging around with. I don't like what's happenin."

I mentioned that Duke was settling down a little—I wanted to give her some relief. Underneath the brave exterior, she seemed very troubled.

"And I don't like the way Duke picks on kids. I think he's reacting to the way the bigger kids pick on him. Do you really think he's getting better?"

She candidly admitted how frustrated she was, stuck in a government-subsidized building, a single parent, out of work. . . . She was feeling stagnant, dormant, even though she was in "the prime of my life."

She found herself weeping in the elevator one day. From crying she went to drinking, gulping tranquilizers and sometimes "running away, leaving Duke alone in the apartment all night." She felt anger against a society that didn't seem to care about her or her son. "Christ, Mr. McLaren, I don't know what I'll do."

Instead of going home directly tonight, I decided I needed to cool myself out: I took a stroll along the boardwalk by the lake, at the foot of my street. I thought about Duke and his mother. Then, restored by the sky and water, I turned towards home.

Thursday, April 28
The lunchroom, which had been created with the intention of serving as a buffer against the hectic classroom, was not always immune to intrusions from the outside world. Just as I was digging into a plate of steaming spaghetti I'd bought at

the nearby Italian restaurant, a gaunt, pock-marked teenager walked into the lunchroom and sat down next to me.

"Are you Ruth's teacher. I'm Jeff—her brother."

I put my fork down. "That's me. How's Ruth been? She's missed most of the week and—"

"Don't know where the hell she is," Jeff said, taking a hand-rolled cigarette from a flat tobacco tin, lighting it.

"What do you mean?"

"Mom took off with Ruth this weekend and said she ain't coming back—ever! My dad figures that maybe mom called you at school. He sent me here to find out."

"I haven't heard a thing." By now, I'd lost my appetite. "Are you sure she won't come back? I mean—has this sort of thing happened before?"

"Mom's always yakkin about leavin and takin Ruth with her if the old man don't get a job. But she's never had the guts."

"If she notifies the school where she is," I said slowly, "the information must be kept confidential. Sorry."

"Ya? Well . . . okay." He rose to his feet and thrust his hands into his back pockets. "Because when the old man catches up with her, he'll kick her ass into tomorrow."

"And what does that mean?" I asked apprehensively.

He cocked a thin, dark eyebrow. "You'll find out, man, you'll find out."

After he left, I asked the secretary to let me know if she receives a letter from another school requesting Ruth's records.

Monday, May 2

Teachers sometimes miss the obvious, even when it stares them in the face every day.

The school year was almost three-quarters over when I noticed that, with very few exceptions, Tina was absent every Monday. I mentioned it to a parent volunteer who lived on the same block as Tina. She looked surprised: "You mean you don't know why Tina misses school on Mondays?"

"No."

"It's the same thing every Monday night," she explained. "Her mother makes her stay home to look after her baby brother during the day. That way it's easier for her mother to sleep all day long. She wants to rest up for the late night session of Bingo."

Well that seemed like a pretty weak reason to keep a kid out of school. I cornered Tina's mother during parent interviews. She was reluctant at first, but eventually she admitted the truth.

"What's one day a week, Mr. McLaren? You tell me! Tina can always make up her school work—just keep her in the next day, after school." She kept raising and lowering her arm, drawing my attention to the fact it was in a cast. "I'm supposed to feel guilty about keepin my daughter home one day a week? You gotta be kiddin! How can I afford a baby-sitter? On a lousy Mother's Allowance cheque I can hardly make the rent! Come on, Mr. McLaren! What's one lousy day a week if Tina makes up for it the next day? Just a drop in the bucket! Look, I got problems. Life ain't easy. My boyfriend's one of them sadists, ya know."

The more she went on, the more crummy I felt.

"How I've managed to take that bastard for almost a year, Lord knows. Take last week," she continued, leaning forward, confidentially. "I ripped the blinkin nail outta my big toe on my son's toy truck, the one I kept tellin him to keep outta the hall. Anyway, I start to scream with pain, but my boyfriend just broke out laughin. The blood was gushin out all over, too." Her face grew more animated as she talked. She began to pantomine the events. "It was my birthday a few days ago. And wouldn't ya know it, he walks in Friday night with no present! And guess what else! You got it—no card, no flowers, no chocolates, no nothin! And the worst part, see, was that I kept remindin him that my birthday was Friday.

"I started yellin and screamin my lungs out. I called him a real creep for comin home drunk as a skunk on my birthday—and nothin in his hands! that's what really threw me! He never even wished me a happy birthday!"

She shook her fist angrily. "Then he tells me he's got me a birthday present. I don't believe him. So he walks up the stairs to where I'm standin, and I'm still rip-roarin mad at him, so he yells 'Here's your birthday present!' and throws me down the stairs!" Which was why her arm was in a cast.

Thursday, May 5

Mrs. Perry is white. She called the school to complain about some black kids in her daughter's reading group. They were calling her daughter names like "slut," "pig" and "vanilla trash."

She asked Rod if her daughter could be put into a group without any black children.

"That's out of the question," Rod replied sternly.

"Why? You got blacks in every single reading group?"

Tuesday, May 10

Sophie wore a limp wreath of straws, strung together from some thread she had picked off the frayed edges of the classroom carpet. On her tee-shirt was printed "Children Are People Too." Her body was bent, emaciated. She walked with her arms across her necklace, as if it were an amulet that would keep her from harm, protecting it from being pulled off.

"I saw Sophie's dad in the elevator last night," Mark suddenly announced to the class. "He was drunk. I know, cause I seen lottsa drunk people before, and when he got out, he fell on the floor."

"You're lyin!" Sophie yelled.

"Sophie's 'welfare,'" Duke taunted. "Your dad's always drunk, ain't he, Sophie?"

"He is not!" cried Sophie, "My dad's sick, that's all! He gots the flu!"

"Then how come his breath stinks?" Duke chimed in, contemptuously. "I was there, too." A flurry of giggles and sniggling passed through the class.

"He wasn't drunk!" Sophie shouted, desperate. "Shut your face!"

"Okay! Okay!" I shouted. "Enough!"

Sophie was already running for the door. Duke reached out and grabbed at her straw necklace as she raced by, breaking it.

"Welfare!" he screamed, as she slammed the door.

Thursday, May 12

Over dinner, I started blaming the entire universe for the problems I was encountering at school: parents, the school system, the government, Western culture in general. I'm becoming quite a cynic. I miss the days when I was a young student radical who really believed society could be changed, poverty abolished, and every one given an equal chance to make something worthwhile of their lives. I've had to grow up.

Was education a middle-class pablum which, upon ingestion, socialized kids into uniform amorphous lumps? It was obvious my kids couldn't fit into the system, so the most obvious solution was to make the system more accommodating to "culturally and economically deprived kids."

"You're putting an educational band-aid over a major social wound," Jenny told me, "when what is really needed is drastic surgery."

I nodded. "But the only people who are empowered to perform the surgery are in top administrative positions, too far away from the scene."

"Become a political activist then,"Jenny suggested, winking.

"Maybe I should," I laughed. "I could go out and try to

abolish poverty and scream about the injustices of the system. Then they might listen enough to give me an executive position on the School Board and ask me to invent a more advanced attendance sheet!"

Friday, May 13

During "news," Dan told the class how his baby sister was run over by a car. She was running across the street to fetch an order of french fries for her mother.

He vividly described how the blood dripped onto the road from her broken nose, and the cut on her head, and the ambulance taking so long to arrive. "I saw her in the hospital today," he told us. "That's why I wasn't here this mornin. My sister's disconscious and talks in her sleep. She talks funny—real slow and shaky like."

"Hey, man, she's drunk," Levon cracked. "What'd she drink—vodka or whiskey?"

"Maybe she was smokin pot," Duke added.

"Wacky tabacky is what my brother calls it," Sandra threw in.

"Hey ... wow!" Jackson said, excited. "I gotta tell my mom! She really likes gory stories!"

"Tell us about the blood!"

By this time I had marched to the front of the room. "Hold it! I don't think Dan finds his sister being hit by a car that exciting!"

"Yah, you guys!" Burt shouted, backing me up. "If you guys find it so neat, why don't you go play on the highway! Go up on the 401 and play in traffic!"

"You guys are gross!" Sandra exclaimed. "I wouldn't wanna watch somebody gettin run over!"

"News is over!" I announced.

Dan walked over to his desk slowly, as if he were measuring each step. He took his seat, put his head down.

"Hey, Dan," Al said, placing his hand on Dan's shoulder. "Keep us posted, eh?"

Monday, May 16

Jabeka sidled up to Marlene's desk and solemnly stated: "Ya know, Marlene, I don't never wanna get married." She usually didn't initiate conversations.

"How come?" Marlene asked.

"You gotta make meals, do the washin, and do whatever the man says. You gotta do the wash on Friday night or Saturday, cause the laundromat's closed on Sundays."

"You don't have to do all that. You and your husband could take turns. I wants to get married when I grows up."

"How come?" it was Jabeka's turn to ask.

"When you gots to pay the rent," Marlene replied smugly, "your husband can pay half."

"My mom gots to do everythin in our house," Jabeka mused. "And she don't like it. Besides, men drinks too much. When they die, you gotta pay a lot of money for their funeral. My grandmother forgots to sign this paper so that the government would pay for my grandfather. He died because he drunk too much, so my grandmother had to pay for buryin him—I member she was real mad. I didn't like my grandfather, he was always drunk. The only time I likes him was at Christmas, when he gave me five dollars."

"Maybe you'll marry a man who don't drinks."

"My mom says that they all drinks too much. Yesterday my mom told me she might get divorced from my dad."

Friday, May 20

The mild weather was my salvation. I took the kids outside to explore the creek at the back of the school. It was ideal for them—they could run around and shout and work off the excess aggression they had built up. When they cooled off, they eagerly tackled the science experiments I had planned.

Duke decided to find a crayfish and write a brief description of it as his project. Unfortunately for the crayfish, his description included a drawing of its insides, which he explored after cutting the crayfish open.

Some of the kids removed their shoes and socks and waded in the creek. That was hazardous, unless you were wearing horseshoes, because of the broken glass and cans and other garbage accumulated over the years. I had to keep a sharp eye on them, warning them away from dangerous areas.

I've started to take my kids outside for more than just science lessons. We enjoy it out there. We set up a little shelter behind some trees, and it becomes our classroom on warm afternoons. We bring our books, papers and pencils with us. The kids use stones as paperweights on windy days to hold their papers in place. Back in class, they decorate the stones, painting them in marvellous colours.

Tuesday, May 24

Max was the school psychologist. He usually showed up on Tuesdays to assess students who had been referred to him by their teachers.

He had read my referral form for a new kid named Matthew, and wanted to see him in a classroom setting. I slipped Max into the back of the room, and the class went on as usual.

Matthew sat at his desk, tapping a book with his pen. His whole body was involved. He shook up and down in a jumping-jack motion, a strange dance in time with the pen taps. The taps were growing louder and louder. He turned and looked at Max. Then he went back to tapping his book—only this time he added some obscene gestures to his act. Matthew's mannerisms were starting to make Max look uncomfortable.

Suddenly Matthew stopped his book-tapping and took three casual steps towards the middle of the room. Then he wildly attacked his desk, pushing it into the corner and turning it completely over, spilling its guts on the floor: pens, pencils, books, binders, loose paper, magic markers I had been searching for for weeks, crayons. . . .

I rushed over to Matthew and grabbed him under the arm. Then I quickly escorted him outside, telling him to stay by the door until he cooled off.

Max agreed to test Matthew. "Once the results are in, though," he said tonelessly, "it may take him years to be placed. There are already so many kids on the waiting list. The system can't absorb them all. Maybe if Matthew's parents were better off and had some pull with the Board. . . ."

On my way out the door tonight, the school secretary told me we'd received a request for Ruth's records from a small, rural school in Alberta.

Friday, May 27

Clad in a pin-stripe suit, plaid vest, and fingering the looping chain of his pocket watch, Fred entered his office, waved me a hello, and slumped down in his Boston rocker.

It was very early in the morning, but already a third of the student body had poured into the library where Dean, the librarian, had set up a special program for kids whose parents worked the early morning shift.

Fingers loosely laced behind his head, Fred kicked off both shoes in one motion, resting his stocking feet on the pine coffee table. He picked up the phone and mumbled a message to his secretary around an unlit cigar.

A tiny black girl in tattered overalls and a baseball cap so large that it almost hid her face timidly knocked on the office door. Fred welcomed her in with a broad grin.

Slowly, almost reluctantly, she removed her hat, revealing a mass of wild dreadlocks that she fingered nervously.

"Who did your hair?" Fred asked, smiling approvingly.

"My auntie," she replied, giving Fred a quick, sideways glance.

"Well then, tell your auntie she did a great job, because you look terrific!"

The girl's head snapped up and her eyes widened. A

smile broke across her face. She rushed across the room and planted a kiss on Fred's forehead. He responded by giving her a long, extended hug.

"She comes in every morning before class," Fred winked, "just to get a hug."

The sincerity of Fred's affection for the kids was obvious. I sometimes wondered whether I was living up to his standards, being only too aware of my lack of love for certain students. Even when I tried looking at the positive side of a particular kid's character—Duke's, for instance—I found it extremely difficult to let go of my hostile feelings. Love couldn't be packaged like a box of curriculum materials and given out by the metric unit—it had to be sincere. Only an affection that was honest and spontaneous would have any effect on the lives of these kids.

Even if it were possible to muster some genuinely warm feelings towards some of the more disruptive kids in my class, how many of them, I wondered, would be able to drop their defences in order to accept it?

When I mentioned this to Fred, he said, "I can get close to the kids because I don't live with thirty-six of them each day as you do. I see them in the halls, or they come and visit me in my office. It's easier for me."

Thursday, June 2
Duke bumper-hitched a ride on my van so many times that today, as I was about to drive off for lunch, I got out and asked him to join me for a hamburger. My suggestion threw him, but after a few seconds he said, "Sure, man, as long as you're buyin."

Around the other kids Duke was aggressive and hard, but often with me he was a completely different person. He talked about missing his dad, spoke eagerly of his plans for a newspaper route. With the money he saved up from his job, he would be able to travel to see his dad—although he admitted sadly that his dad never wrote him or his mom.

Duke and I agreed to have more excursions for hamburgers, but from now on, he says, he'll pay for his own.

Monday, June 6

"Wanna know somethin, sir?" Jabeka asked out of the blue.

"Sure. What's on your mind?"

"My step-dad went to Jamaica last night for good. He wants me to go with him, but I didn't want to. So he took my brother instead."

"Why's your step-dad leaving?"

"My mom don't like him no more. Me either! You know, when he buys us clothes they're always old, and they tear easy. When they go in the washin machine, they shrinks."

"Is that all?"

"No, sir. When I was a little baby he changed my diapers and treated me real rough."

"Can you remember that far back, Jabeka?"

"Well, my mom told me."

"What else did she say?"

"When I was a little girl, I had a bleedin nose and was chokin and my step-dad just put on his coat and went to a party. And after the party he went to sleep in the park."

"Aren't you going to miss your step-dad, though?"

"No! But I'll miss my brother. My mom kicked my step-dad out for good, after last week."

"What happened last week?"

"My step-dad gave me a grown-up pill, and I started to cough. There was a pin stuck in it!"

"Don't you ever want to see him again?"

"Just at Christmas, so's he can give me lots of presents. He told me he was goin to spend lots of money on me!"

Wednesday, June 8

In the first months of my Master's course, I read all the classic theorists: Dewey, Piaget, Bruner.... At the same time, I was beginning to realize that my best teaching days were those in which I put aside theory and simply allowed things to happen spontaneously. Some lessons were disasterous, but mostly they worked.

What worked best, I discovered, was bringing in art materials, reading kits, musical instruments, woodworking tools, and so forth—and letting the kids handle these materials with a minimum of supervision.

Sometimes I'd try to channel what they were doing into conventional subjects. For instance, measuring lumber for a classroom clubhouse could be a math lesson in itself. Cleaning up the creek that ran behind the school became a lesson in ecology.

The important thing was to develop what I call a "caring patience." It was so easy to get frustrated with the kids; it was easy to hate them at times. But if you waited long enough, and tried to give them the benefit of the doubt, you couldn't help loving them—well, most of them.

And the kids became more affectionate, too. Sometimes they'd give me a hug or a kiss—that is, the girls would. The boys showed their affection in other ways. Levon and Duke built me a pair of bookends.

Friday, June 10

There was a loud knock on the door. I opened it and was met by three grim women. The heaviest one, in a pink bathrobe with kitty fluff around the collar, carried a baseball bat. They were, in inner-city lingo, "headhunters."

"Where's Mr. Hartford's room?" the heavy one demanded in a raspy voice, adjusting her robe so that it covered her enormous cleavage.

"Down the hall to your left," I replied. "Is there a problem?"

"One of my kids told me that Mr. Hartford roughed up my littlest one, Tony, at recess. And believe me, I'm gonna make him pay!"

"I'll show you where his room is," I said nervously. "But I'm sure there must be some mistake."

We went down the hall together.

"Hart" was the school "heavy." He turned to face us, squaring his great shoulders. He was leaning against the wall, his massive arms folded over his Budweiser belt buckle.

"What's this about you slappin Tony around at recess, Hartford?" the lady with the bat demanded.

"Are you his mother?"

"That's right! An I want an explanation!"

"I suppose you were informed that Tony was in a fight at recess and was kicking another boy in the face when he was down? I had to grab Tony and pull him off the kid. Is that a good enough explanation?"

"I didn't hear it that way," the lady responded, looking a bit puzzled.

"There was another teacher on yard duty who can back me up. Do you want me to call her?" Hart asked.

"Forget it," the lady said. "Come on, girls!" she barked. "Let's go home. Somebody's been lyin to me, and I'll be using this bat yet!"

Monday, June 13

Sir! I gots a rotten tooth! It wiggles and this gooey stuff leaks out!

It's just spit. Lemmie knock it out for ya!

I think you should see the school dentist, Levon. You'd better hurry before he leaves for the day.

No way. That dentist is a Paki!

Well, you're a nigger! Haaaaa!

Look! I've already spoken to you about using words like that!

A Paki is a Paki no matter what you say!

I gots this big pimple under my chin!

I'll punch that out too! I'll give you an uppercut!

Go jerk off, why don't you!

Hey sir, can I whisper you a secret?

What is it, Dan?

Only if you promise not to tell Duke.

Okay. What is it?

Duke and I went to this movie on the weekend . . . right?

Right.

So we sits down near the back to watch the show. Then this chick sits down a few seats away . . . right?

Right.

Duke sits next to her and puts this popcorn box on his lap. The box is all empty . . . right?

Right.

So he takes the bottom off the box—just rips it away. Then he puts the box over his thing . . . right?

Go on.

Then he says to the chick, "Want some popcorn?" The chick says, "Sure," so she reaches into the box . . .

Good God!

Sir! Duke's tryin to break my pimple!

Okay class! Settle down! You've still got your stories to finish off before recess.

I don't feel like doin a story!

Hey . . . why don't you leave sir alone. His face is grey. Can't you tell he's constipated?

Wednesday, June 15

My first official reprimand from Fred occurred when I started a school newspaper. Poems, stories and drawings were collected on stencils submitted by all the grades, from kindergarten right through to grade six. It was all done in a rush.

The secretary spent the entire day running them off. We sold about three hundred copies for five cents each, which paid for the paper. All the kids took them home.

Unfortunately, my proofreading turned out to be far from perfect. After most of the papers were sold, Fred pointed out that I had overlooked a "Paki joke" one kid had submitted. I felt very bad about it, and was very careful in the future about what went into the paper.

However, there were no complaints from the parents about the "joke."

Monday, June 20

On the weekend, snipers fired rifles from the roofs of nearby high-rises. I found a bullet hole in the front door of the school.

At the dinner table my wife almost choked on her food when I told her about it. I tried to calm her down. "It was probably just a bunch of teenagers playing a prank. There's nothing for the kids to do in the area," I said. "Sometimes they get so damn bored and frustrated they choose rather bizarre outlets."

"That's no excuse for people taking pot-shots at build-ings," Jenny protested. "One day somebody's going to get hurt—seriously hurt!"

"Look Jenny, kids are kids. I remember growing up in the suburbs myself. My friends and I used to do some pretty wild things on occasions. I had this B.B. gun once and we took it down to the golf course and fired it at the fence posts—"

"Fence posts and B.B. guns are one thing, real guns are another. Maybe I'm naive, but what the kids in that area need are some decent recreational facilities, youth clubs, a sense of purpose. And what kind of community is that to grow up in? Everything looks the same—all the shopping plazas, the high-rises, the townhouses, the parking lots. I grew up in the suburbs, too, don't forget. The corner store, the milkman, the fire hall—they were always there. Today the kids can go to the corner store and a week later it's been torn down and a sprawling mall is put up in its place. And all the stories you come home with about your kids . . . it really scares me. You know that they're not going to get through high school—to say nothing of college. Most of them are being programmed to be losers. I know we've talked about this before, and don't get that look on your face, but why don't you take a job somewhere else? I hate to see you come home so depressed all the time; you're going to get ulcers. Thank God you don't drink seriously or you'd be heading for the alcoholic ward by now."

"Somebody's got to teach these kids," I said. "As a matter of fact, it's *these* kids that need the best teachers. You were the one that said that, even before I took the job, remember? By the way, there was a job posting on the bulletin board today—teaching gifted kids out in the east end. I thought about applying for it for a while, but changed my mind. Look, there's got to be a solution to make life a little better for these kids. I've got to keep trying."

"Promise me one thing."

"What's that?"

"You won't let this job interfere with our life."

I took a deep breath. "Okay. When I start bringing my job home with me after school every day, I'll think about transferring—or something. But really, that's a long way off."

"I hope so, honey. And I *do* know how you feel about the kids and how they need you."

"And in some strange way that I don't understand, I need them."

Wednesday, June 22

I was late getting my final report cards finished and went into a mild panic. I tried to work on them during class, but it was much too noisy. I even tried to work on them during yard duty, but that, of course, was doomed to failure.

During lunch, John noticed all my report cards spread out in front of me. He said I bore a strong resemblance to a newscaster who had just thrown an epileptic seizure. So I explained.

"When the noise in my room gets too much," he told me, "I simply throw the kids a test. That usually shuts them up for at least half an hour!"

Of course! I hurried into the office, grabbed a handful of stencils, drew up a math test, and quickly ran it off on the machine.

While I worked on my report cards, the class worked steadily on their test. Until, that is, Janice shouted, "Duke threw a magazine out the window!"

I let the incident go by in favour of peace and quiet. "No talking," I said. "Keep your mind on the test!"

Next, the door was kicked open and Karen somersaulted into the room. Her mother outside bellowed, "Get into that room! Don't you try and tell *me* you're sick!"

Shortly afterwards, the recess bell sounded. I hurried over to the main building for a cigarette.

When I returned I noticed a crowd of tiny kindergarten kids gathered around a torn magazine outside my portable. I took a closer look.

On the cover was a nude and bloodied woman with mammoth breasts. She was bound by several studded leather straps, spread-eagled to a chair. Headlined over the picture was "Man rapes woman with boyfriend's bleeding head."

"Wow!" I heard one of the kids whisper.

Thursday, June 23
Now that the year was nearly over, I noticed that Duke had mellowed considerably, almost to the point where I wondered whether his toughness wasn't simply bravado all along.

It couldn't be disputed that he displayed a savagery, certainly a sadism, in several fights I witnessed. But the fighting seemed to be happening less frequently now.

Last fall he had forced a kid named Lindsay to eat a piece of dog crap. Now he was acting more the benevolent despot. Since he no longer initiated fights, neither did his followers. He swore off smoking, so smoking became taboo. He took up gymnastics after school, and his gang dutifully practised their somersaults on the gym mats.

One teacher told me she spotted Duke signing out a book from the library—if true, what a precedent!

Wednesday, June 29

Rod had been asked by a Board trustee if the school could contribute some children's artwork to the Canada Day celebration at the nearby junior-high school. Knowing more than a little Board politics, he agreed. Our school, he decided, would have the best display of the festival. I was to coordinate the exhibit, gathering together murals and paintings by the students which emphasized Canada as the land of opportunity, multiculturalism, solidarity, happiness and wonderful community spirit.

Everybody showed up for the celebrations: parents, school trustees, social workers in denim overalls, red-nosed alkies, cops, glazed-eyed teenagers, senior citizens.

Buddy showed up, too. Within three minutes, my cassette tape recorder was missing. I called him over and asked if he'd like to play detective for me. He replied succinctly: "Go shovel shit, Mr. McLaren."

Then I politely asked if he'd like to reconsider playing Sherlock Holmes, only this time offering a five dollar reward. Buddy smiled. "Sure, Mr. McLaren. I'm gonna be a detective when I grows up. I'll get it back."

About five minutes later Buddy returned. The tape recorder was tucked under his arm, and there was a big grin on his face. "I caughts this son-of-a-bitch runnin off with it

to the plaza. So I runs after him, and tells him to give it back. When I caughts up to him, I says it belongs to Mr. McLaren, this real nice teacher friend of mine, so he'd better hand it over." Buddy could have easily surpassed Sherlock Holmes by simply solving only the crimes he himself committed.

I shouldn't have reinforced Buddy's theft by giving him a reward, but I needed my tape recorder for the celebrations.

Unfortunately, the festivities were cancelled shortly after they began. Too many tires were being slashed in the parking lot (including the police cruisers), the lady that ran the dunking pool had her purse stolen, and one of the policemen on duty "lost" his hat!

O Canada!

Epilogue

Congratulations were heaped on me by the administration—I had survived the year.

Although little learning in the strict academic sense seemed to have taken place, the kids did pick up some skills. But I was still too conditioned by Teacher's College to feel I had accomplished what was expected of me—that is, providing the kids with an "education" as outlined in the Ministry of Education guidelines. I wanted to use all the curriculum materials I had collected but, somehow, there never seemed to be the time.

I threw a party for the kids, and they did a beautiful job of decorating the portable; it was a crepe-paper paradise. I felt it the best atmosphere to make my farewell.

The fun was cut short when Buddy floated by to check out the music. He wanted to be the disc-jockey, but Muscle Lady was challenging him for the job. To avoid a confrontation, I decided to take the kids over to the gym, where a larger graduation dance was just beginning.

All the young calypsonians were there: feet were tapping and hips were swaying to the beat of West Indian reggae. Scores of kids crammed into the gym, dancing as they came through the door. A mass of swirling bodies, arms upraised in celebration describing graceful arcs, heads thrown back in blissful abandonment, they slowly gravitated towards the stage. There they were met by a multitude of other revellers, knees buckling, feet shuffling, hips rolling to a street-wise boogie.

Muscle Lady whirled onto the stage amid a pulsing strobe light, lip-synching her theme song, *Vibrations,* her bare legs revealed through her translucent pants.

Buddy stood in the middle of the floor, his shiny black hair reflected by the light as sharp criss-crossed wires. He danced wildly, with a covey of onlookers applauding.

"There's my man!"

"Watch him move, ladies!"

"Hang it all out!"

"Shake those feet!"

He smiled back, obviously enjoying the spotlight. Everybody was having a great time.

The next day there was a staff meeting. When I heard that a grade four class was being vacated by a teacher who was transferring, I asked if I could take the class; Fred agreed. I loved my kids, but felt frustrated; the thought nagged at me that I wasn't helping them enough.

I suppose I expected a feeling of elation or accomplishment at the end of the year, some kind of emotional ovation. I had come through a long period of fragmentation, and now I was ready for a "quantum leap" towards sanity. All year it had been as if I had been homesteading on the frontiers of despair. I had changed from a relatively even-tempered and reasonably patient person into a mass of raw nerve endings and brute instinct. I had formed a protective shell around my emotions in a desperate attempt to keep myself from being drawn into the deeply wounded lives of the kids.

I had been too idealistic. I wanted the classroom to be a place where the whole would contribute to the health of its parts. I wanted to show the kids how to express their conflicts without tormenting each other. I suppose in a sense I had achieved some of my aims. After all, the kids did express their feelings. But with all the role-playing, psychodrama and class discussions, I had expected greater harmony.

For most of their lives, school for these kids had been a kind of enforced lethargy, where violence became the natural culture of the classroom. I wanted to change the kids' perception of school, to free them from everything about learning that seem so mechanical: bells keeping kids in step and on time, curriculums plotting out each separate skill to be learned, and when.

I didn't want to be just a PR man probing the fractured psyches of the kids in the name of achievement and competition; I wanted to mend some of the tears in their emotional lives. But in attempting to do so, I was becoming an emotional wreck myself. It was almost impossible to teach kids who were emotionally unstable and who possessed self-concepts that barely came up to ground level. Too many of the kids felt like rodents in a locked cage, fed crumbs by strangers, and from which there was no escape. I had seen sporadic, impulsive and ultimately senseless violence with very few strands of hope.

The questions I asked myself over and over were: What kind of person had I really been to the kids? How much did I help them negotiate with their world?—to me, the essence of education. A public school teacher has the heavy responsibility of helping kids negotiate with all kinds of things: language, geography, art, drama, gym, reading, film, mathematics, social skills—and making them relevant to the world outside. At the very least I should be able to help them get along with each other, or so I thought.

I debated whether or not to attend a summer course at University that might provide me with some ammunition. But Jenny insisted that what I really needed was a break from anything to do with teaching. So we took out a loan from the credit union and packed our bags for San Francisco. I hadn't been there since my visit in the sixties, and I looked forward to seeing that beautiful city again. The change of scenery and the chance to put my job out of my mind would be welcome.

But on the trip home I started thinking about the kids again: I couldn't put them out of my thoughts. My mind was filled with so many unanswered questions: Would the younger kids in grade four be more enthusiastic and less defiant of authority? Could I reach them before they were conditioned to be so defiant and have such low opinions of themselves? Could school be more than just an expensive babysitting service?

My new class would be in the main building, actually the largest room in the school, the former library. When some kids had set fire to the building, the new wing was built, leaving the old library unoccupied.

A classroom would have many advantages over the portable. A delightful thought occurred: I wouldn't freeze in winter each time I had to go to the bathroom. Most of my boys, rather than trudge to the main building, preferred to urinate in the snow outside the portable. It was an experience, having a gallery of yellow abstracts to gaze on. There must have been an art to it, since I definitely appreciated some more than others. Sometimes I'd walk by a row of "angels" that the kids had made by lying in the snow and flapping their arms and legs. All my "angels" had yellow eyes and yellow mouths. When I began to recognize individual artists by their style, I knew it was time to find an inside classroom.

So now, I would have a brand-new grade four class to tackle. During our holiday I had sought spiritual refuge in books, to get "psyched up" for the following year. I also picked up some books on alternative schools and progressive teaching techniques from the local library.

At home, full of excitement, I energetically searched for the grade four programs I had from Teacher's College. I discovered I had used them to keep the refrigerator level.

The
Invisible
Epidemic

2

Friday, September 2

This morning I decided to get a head start on the term. I arrived at my "new" room to find chairs piled haphazardly on desks that had been pushed into a heap in the corner. The bulletin boards were still littered with debris left by the previous teacher, and old torn posters still hung on the walls.

Rather than put the desks into straight rows as I had done the previous year, I decided to arrange them in rectangular groups of six each. I dragged in a few tables from the stockroom and set up the art centre near the sink. I also acquired a broken tape-recorder as an improvement for my "sound centre." It complemented the record player and earphones.

My biggest challenge, I had learned, would not be in teaching the kids—my biggest challenge would not be in getting along with the other teachers—my biggest challenge would be in trying to please the caretakers!

They had insisted last year that I put my desks back into rows at the end of a day, because that way it was easier to sweep my room at night. And then, when I brought in some old furniture I had found down at the Sally Ann, they refused to help me carry it upstairs. They protested that my classroom was already a junkheap!

I found Rod in his office and asked him if I could borrow a TV for my room; there were three TV sets circulating. The one I asked for had a broken stand and was usually left idle in the stockroom. Teachers were unlikely to ask for it because it was large and heavy and a big pain to move. No one would get upset about me monopolizing *that* set! And maybe it would keep my class quiet after lunch when kids were usually at their rowdiest.

Rod helped me move the set to my room (I didn't bother asking the caretakers—how much rejection could I take?) and I checked out the educational programs that were showing.

Tuesday, September 6

On the first day of class, I talked to the kids about the kind of program I wanted to run.

"Are we gonna to do any sports?" one student asked.

"Floor hockey?"

"I don't like floor hockey, sir," a tall kid offered, rising slightly out of his desk.

"What kind of sport do you like?" I asked, tensing.

He jerked his thumb at the lapel of his shirt. The button he wore read: "Canadian Breast Stroking Champion." "That's me!" he declared, grinning.

Friday, September 9

I had promised the kids we'd watch TV this morning. I settled on a program called "Cover to Cover" about children's books, with an artist illustrating the stories. The class sat and watched the show quietly. I was beaming.

As soon as the set was turned off, however, the kids became more hyperactive than ever! Somehow, TV activates a child. It creates a reaction in the child to the TV images—but during the program, the child sits quietly, watching, without any way of releasing all of the energy that is slowly building up. By the time the show was over and the TV was turned off, my kids' batteries were fully charged, and they were rowdier than ever!

I sadly reported to Rod that my TV experiment wasn't working out, and that I was going to return the set to the stockroom. One of the caretakers happened by and over-heard us. "Hey McLaren! I'd be happy to lug that TV back to stockroom for you!" he volunteered, smiling.

The only time the caretaker ever did me a favour was when it involved taking something *out* of my room!

Monday, September 12
My new inside location has a definite drawback—the wash-room, conveniently situated just around the corner, has proven more popular than my classroom.

A steady stream of kids clutching their groins, hopping up and down, continually line up at the door waiting to be excused. Or three or four kids make a mad dash for the washroom without bothering to ask for permission. It got so bad I was forced to actually move my desk in front of the door to control the situation.

Then groups of kids complained about the continual noise in the classroom, and asked if they could do their seat-work in the hall. I reluctantly agreed, setting a limit of five kids at any time for my "hall group." Every five minutes or so I peeked out to check on them. So far, so good.

This afternoon I noticed whenever I checked that there were always some kids missing. When I asked where they were, the others simply shrugged their shoulders and ex-claimed, "They're with the other freaks!"

"Other freaks?"

"Card freaks!" they shouted, and pointed to the end of the hall.

Down the hall a group of about twenty kids from different classrooms was huddled together in the stairwell tossing hockey cards against the wall. It was such a serious competition I felt a little guilty when I broke up the game and sent them all back to their classes.

Wednesday, September 14

It would drive anyone a little crazy. At least half the class wandered around the room at any given time, despite my attempts to keep them working quietly at their desks. The constant movement was threatening.

Relief happily appeared with Hartford, the gym teacher, who took my kids twice a week for half-hour sessions.

Usually I ended up chatting with a small group of kids who had forgotten their gym equipment and remained behind. It was the same group every week, a coincidence, I'm sure. I looked forward to my half-hour raps with these kids, nick-naming them "the rap pack." I dreamed of what it would be like to have a class with only six or seven students. There were kids in the "rap pack" whom I could barely tolerate in a normal classroom with thirty-five students. But individually or in the small group, they were easy to talk to, sensitive and communicative.

When the rest of the class returned from the gym, the "rap pack" reverted to their former selves: distant, rowdy, anti-social.

Friday, September 16

Behavioural modification was a term I was introduced to in Teacher's College. So when it came up as a topic at an "inner-city" professional development day conference, I wasn't a bit surprised.

"Behavioural mod is what you need to marshall these inner-city toughs in line," I was advised. One teacher described the "check system" to me, so I decided to try it out.

I stripped the bulletin boards on both sides of my room, and tacked up the names of all thirty-five of my pupils along the top. Under each name, I hammered in five nails forming a vertical straight line, spaced so that five pie plates could be punched and hung from the nails. Each pie plate stood for one day. One side of a pie plate was a happy face. The other side, a frown.

After explaining the rules to the class, I showed how I could turn over a pie plate to the frown if the child sinned. If one of my kids sinned twice, I could put a sticker on the plate. Five stickers meant the child had six checks against him or her. If a kid managed to go the entire week with only one check, he or she received a pack of gum and "free activity time." They cheered at that, of course. But if he or she managed to get zapped more than three times in any single day, then the culprit had to stay after school and do extra work from my "sad face" book.

But there was still more.

When I yelled "Carpet check!," the kids had to run over to the carpeted area and sit down. "Sound check!" meant that all the kids had to sit quietly and listen. "Desk check!" meant that all the kids should rush to their little desks. We all agreed to try it.

"Okay kids!" I began. "Carpet check!"

They all ran over each other rushing to the carpet, and knocking down a little girl in the process. Her lip started to bleed a little. While I made sure she was okay, I said "Sound check!," and everyone quieted down. Which was when Elvin stood up: "I don't like this game!"

"Check for Elvin!" I said at once.

Eddie, my newly chosen "check monitor," promptly took Monday's pie plate and turned it to the sad face.

"Class," I said, "the first check of the year goes to Elvin!"

I was suddenly overwhelmed with every kid demanding they get checks, too! Somehow, they had gotten things mixed up. I tried explaining the system all over again. Confident, I sent the kids back to their desks with a resounding "Desk check!"

After enough time had passed for the kids to finish their assignment, I called "Carpet check!" Thirty-five pairs of assorted sneakers pattered to the rug.

Wait a minute! It was only thirty-four pairs!

I heard fuming and muttering at the back of the room. T.J. was still at his desk, mumbling angrily. T.J. wasn't going to cooperate. Why should he? He was most at home in chaos, not order. The other kids would follow his lead if I didn't do something—and quick.

T.J. was staring at the ceiling, arms folded defiantly across his chest, his red woollen beret pulled over one eye. Then he started to get up. I felt a surge of confidence. Then slowly he slunk back into his chair, glaring at me. Then, he stuck out his tongue. Everyone waited for me to make my move.

"Stay at your desk!" I told him, as if I had wanted him there all along. "Open your book!"

This strategy caught him off guard. He started to open his speller, then suddenly slammed it shut, his eyes squinting. "You sucker! You ain't getting T.J. to the rug! Not that way! You gimmie some gum like everybody else is gonna get! Eh, eh? Then I'll go! But you ain't keepin me in! I got to get right home after school cause I gotta go for a blood test!"

"You'll get your gum just like everybody else if you follow the rules!"

"I want a promise!" he demanded.

"Uh ... well ... if you've got a good reason not to stay in, I'll look into it."

Suddenly there was a room full of excuses. "I can't stay in either, sir, cause my mom's takin me to Towers to get me some socks!" Betsy had to take her younger cousin right home after school. Murray had "sore tonsils," and maybe the doctor would want to "cut em out" after school. And so on.

I was panic-stricken. I started checking everybody: "Check T.J.! Check Winston! Check Murray! Check Betsy! Double-check Betsy!"

But Eddie, my loyal check monitor, protested louder than the others. "I can't stay in either, sir, or my dad will beat me! I have to look after my little brother!"

"Check yourself, Eddie!" I groaned in despair.

The next day, I told the class we were going back to our normal routine. T.J. told everyone it was because I was too cheap to buy gum.

Tuesday, September 20

Melissa wore a plastic charm with the signs of the zodiac around her neck. It was a good-luck token for her mother, who was dying of cancer. She clutched it tightly, and sometimes shoved it under her sweater so it rested next to her skin.

The day after her mother died, Melissa ripped the pendant from her neck and threw it out the window.

Wednesday, September 21

During the first few weeks in class, Sal had a gentle manner that lulled me into complacency. There was no way this kid could ever give me problems in class; it was simply out of the question. On the surface, he was all friendly gestures, eagerness and ambition.

This afternoon Sal was sitting quietly at his desk, fingers laced behind his neck, leaning back in his seat. The kid beside him called him a name—some innocuous remark, like "goof-ball."

He reared back with a sideways look and threw his desk against the wall with a crash! He sprang growling at the kid, seizing him by the neck and screaming, "Fuck right off, why don't ya!" Then he violently brought his chin down on the kid's head.

Flesh tore. Blood gushed like a tiny geyser down into his eyes. The kid's face twisted into a mask of horror. In the few seconds before I pulled him away, Sal sent a flurry of kicks into the kid's ribs.

I grabbed Sal under the arms and spun him around, forcing him back to his desk. He watched me guardedly, his head lowered. Then his wild, angry face suddenly melted into a little boy's ingratiating grin.

"Lost my cool, eh sir?"

The class, which had remained silent, now sputtered and giggled. Two boys took the wounded victim downstairs, while my gentle, friendly Sal pushed his hair back from his face, grinning.

Tuesday, September 27

Professional development days are traditionally set aside to allow teachers to attend lectures, conferences and workshops to keep up with the latest developments in education. For us, it really meant a welcome day of relief from the kids.

Most inner-city teachers I talked with found the PD lectures irrelevant. It was pretty hard—but relaxing, compared with teaching the kids—to wait out the boredom of the lecture so we could all go out together for a good lunch.

The "Halfway House" restaurant at Pioneer Village was the most popular eating spot for PD lunches. I think the staff enjoyed the walk through Pioneer Village, an exact replica of a Canadian town in the 1800s, as much as the meal itself. It was such a stark contrast to the bleak surroundings of the Corridor.

After listening to a particularly boring lecture, Hartford whispered in my ear: "Let's skip Pioneer Village and go to the Golden Star for a beer!"

After the lecture, Hart and I rounded up Big Arnie and Mrs. Rogers, piled into Hart's stationwagon and drove off to the Golden Star.

As Hart led us to a table at the front of the tavern, Mrs. Rogers pointed to the stripper on stage, remarking, "I hope my womens' consciousness-raising group doesn't find out about this!"

The stripper, a lithe blonde in her teens, had almost finished her gyrations by the time we took our seats. Hart's eyes were glued on her final bumps and grinds as the music on the juke box slowly faded. After a bit more scrutiny he thumped his fist on the table. "I knew it! That's Cathy Huston up there!"

"Cathy who?"

"Cathy Huston!" Hart said emphatically. "I'm sure of it." A look of surprise and bewilderment covered his face. "I taught Cathy in grade six."

I watched his face turn red as the stripper, her act completed, now covered herself with a black lace negligee. She made her way across the room in the direction of our table. When she got to us, she stopped and looked down at Hart, puzzled, while he sat there stone-faced. Then she smiled.

"Hiya, Hartford!"

"Hiya, Cathy," Hart managed. She then went past our table and disappeared into a room behind the bar. We all just sort of sat there. Hart cleared his throat. "Uh . . . anybody want to try the roast beef at Pioneer Village?" he finally asked. "We've still got an hour left."

We quietly finished off our beers and left.

Wednesday, October 5

Jenny mentioned last night that I seemed to be losing much of my enthusiasm so early in the term. She'd noticed that I didn't spend as much time preparing lessons, and I avoided discussing school events. I couldn't give her a ready answer, and it worried me. After mulling it out, I finally decided to discuss it with Fred.

I told him that I felt helpless, ineffective. My rookie enthusiasm seemed on the wane. No longer a neophyte, I felt I should be making much more progress with the kids. The signs of physical and emotional abuse that the kids brought to class from their homes and the incidents of violence I had witnessed in class all seemed to be part of the normal state of affairs, rather than isolated incidents. Isolated pockets of classroom disturbances I could handle . . . react to . . . follow up on. But it was another matter to be confronted with a situation where every day, all thirty-five pupils seemed to be out of control. How could I possibly establish a close relationship with so many kids?

I thought about the books and articles I had read on disadvantaged kids. In most of them, the authors wrote about problem kids in special classes, with one teacher to every ten kids. Now that seemed reasonable. But life in my class was like being machine-gunned by events so quickly that it was impossible to keep track of everything. I was feeling numbed, insensitive, apathetic.

Fred's answer was so simple, I couldn't believe it, yet it had tremendous impact on me. He told me that although I should try to reach as many kids as possible, that if I only affected a single kid in my entire class, my presence would have been worthwhile. He told me to relax, and not have such high expectations.

"This is the only way you can keep your spirits up," he said. "If you're going to worry about not reaching every kid, you won't reach any. If you tell yourself that if something positive happens with a kid, no matter how small it seems, that it's worthwhile, well then you'll do fine. You'll be in shape emotionally to help that next kid who's standing in line."

Wednesday, October 12

Unless some miracle intervenes, I'll have T.J. in my class for the rest of the year. My fellow teachers admire me greatly for taking him on. Two years older than the other kids, by the time he'd hit grade four his records were thick with reports of classroom disruption.

T.J. is painfully thin, with the narrowest face imaginable and a shrill, bleating voice. His skin is stretched over his tiny head like a Hallowe'en mask. He continually spews a steady stream of obscenities from thin lips that are covered with rose-coloured sores.

As soon as I saw him scurry about the class, gouging victims with pencil swipes, I knew I was in for trouble. When I asked him over to my desk for a friendly chat, he refused to move from his desk, held there by some unnatural gravity that affected only T.J., but none of the other kids.

At ten, T.J. is the second youngest in a family of eleven criminals. Everyone has police records, including his parents. The one exception is his six-year-old brother, Mickey.

This afternoon, while I was having lunch at T.J.'s, the police came in and arrested his second eldest brother for assault. Mickey ran after the police cruiser shouting: "You fuckin pigs! Bastards! Bring my brother back!"

Lunch at T.J.'s is always eventful. The grey arborite kitchen table is the family's focus; here they spend most of the day eating, smoking, arguing and getting stoned.

Imitation wooden plaques on the wall bear inscriptions such as:

Old fishermen never die
They just smell that way

Old golfers never die
They just lose their balls

Eat, drink and be merry
For tomorrow you may diet

Lining the windowsill above the sink are bowling trophies, plants in pink flamingo vases, the complete collection of Red Rose Tea china miniatures, and a toy model of an outhouse which features a plastic figurine urinating through a crescent-shaped hole in the door, a present from T.J.'s grandparents who live in a small farming community near London, Ontario.

T.J. loves his grandparents. He loves to visit his grandfather. Sometimes in class he tells me stories of going to visit him in his step-dad's metallic green pickup truck, complete with whitewall tires. He'd show off the body work and pinstriping to "gramps" and let him feel the broadloomed dash. Gramps promised T.J. he'd buy him one of those toy dogs whose eyes burn red when the brake lights are on. T.J. wishes he could move in with his grandparents.

His unusually tall, wolf-faced mother always seems anxious. She directs the kitchen chaos in an orange negligee covered with black "happy face" designs, held together at the waist by a green tie (part of a security guard's uniform belonging to her ex-husband—the company monogram was stitched on the front of it).

Mickey, the younger brother, shoved a wall calendar into my hands that he'd stolen from his sister's house— pornographic. All of the sister's up-coming court dates had been pencilled in, and they ran through to next year.

T.J.'s mother told me she had hopes that T.J. would be the "black sheep" of the family—that is, the only offspring *not* to turn to crime. But her hopes were swiftly disappearing. T.J. keeps getting into trouble. It looks as if there's little that can be done about it. He's already been in court once for throwing gasoline at the mailboxes of a nearby high-rise and then setting them on fire. Fortunately, the blazes were quickly doused.

T.J.'s mother wanted me to drop by after school tomorrow to celebrate the release of her eldest son's best friend from the hospital. There was going to be lots of beer, chips, and Dolly Parton on the record player. The friend, who had been in a motorcycle accident, had been sitting behind the driver when they crashed suddenly into the rear-end of a car. The driver's thigh bone popped out from its socket and shot backwards, puncturing the friend's left testicle.

T.J.'s mom commented: "In this life, you can still get by with one ball, as long as your pecker's all in one piece!"

Friday, October 14

When I went to public school, the worst you coud be was the classroom tattle-tale. Squealing on somebody—anybody— was an outrage. Even among the very young, loyalty to the pack went unspoken. So I was totally dumbfounded by the casual way Elvin betrayed the other kids in the class.

"Sir," Elvin began one morning, "Eddie's got two boxes of crayons in his desk instead of one. He stole one pack from your desk. I know 'cause I saw him do it."

Or, "Sir, I saw Betsy take an extra pencil from your filing cabinet. I saw her with my very own eyes."

He would even squeal on *me*!

"Hey, guess what?" one day he asked the class. "I saw sir put a box of thumbtacks in his briefcase. I bet he stole em for his kid!!"

The class ate it up.

That did it!

I borrowed a slang term used in prisons for stool pigeons: "wearing the snitch jacket." The next day I brought in one of my more beat-up jackets. The idea was to make Elvin put it on each time he finked on somebody. The kids thought it was a lark. Everybody started to snitch on their friends just to be able to put the jacket on and ham it up for the rest of the class!

I quietly took the snitch jacket home.

Monday, October 17

Big Arnie, formerly a kindergarten teacher, had been hired as the school's new "compensatory" teacher—he was responsible for setting up a classroom to accommodate groups of kids who found it difficult to function in regular classroom settings.

Arnie offered miniature hockey, table tennis, darts, macramé, lessons on how to use a yo-yo (Arnie was an expert), and colouring Star Wars stencils. He also served as a sounding board for the kids' problems.

Teachers would choose up to five kids from a class, and send them over to Arnie for half an hour at a time. Some teachers used the opportunity to go to Arnie's room as a bribe, so kids would finish their work. Other teachers admitted sending kids to Arnie that they didn't like—just to get them out of the room. Teachers are only human.

But one of his pet projects always failed. Arnie, quite overweight, planned monthly weight-loss contests for the staff. He brought in scales, set up graphs. Teachers who participated put five dollars into the "pot," and the teacher who lost the most weight kept the pot at the end of the month.

Big Arnie never won.

Friday, October 21

The local community centre was offering soup-and-sandwich lunches for a dollar, so I went over. Who could beat that price?

While munching on a tasty hot sandwich, I met a beautiful West Indian woman named Saffron, who had a background of social work in Jamaica and was presently doing some volunteer work, counselling teenagers in our area. She started to talk about the fate of many West Indian youngsters coming into the country.

"The usual pattern is for West Indian immigrants to leave their children behind with relatives. When the parent finds a job, she—they're usually single mothers—sends for her kids. It's easy to leave kids back home temporarily, because there's always a big family, with aunts, cousins and grandparents ready to take a child in.

"Many times, the mother marries again and starts a new family. When her children finally arrive from the Islands, they not only have to cope with a new culture, but with a new daddy."

Talking with her put the situation of one of my students into some perspective. Rhonda's brother, Leroy, had recently come from Jamaica to join her, their mom and a new step-father. Rhonda had joined her mother a year earlier. The transition had gone well, and Rhonda enjoyed living in Canada: she did well at school.

Her brother, on the other hand, took an instant dislike to his step-father. Leroy was placed in Mrs. Rogers' class at school, and immediately was at odds with the other kids. During the first week, he pummelled one of his classmates after being called a "black bastard."

A few weeks later, he was caught shoplifting from the nearby plaza and charged by the police.

Monday, October 31

After we saw a slide show on West Indian culture, two of my West Indian girls asked if they could braid my hair.

Charleen, very hyperactive, and always in the throes of a high-strung dance, leaned a rickety shoulder into my back and started working on the crown of my head.

She put the comb through my hair, twisting it tightly, and winding it round and round. My hair became hopelessly entangled in the comb.

Rhonda had to get the scissors and cut the comb out.

T.J. lent me his Blue Jays cap until I got used to how ridiculous I looked.

Tuesday, November 1

When the kids asked me if they could play some music for the last half hour each day, I agreed reluctantly. They might get out of control, but it was worth the risk; music was an important part of their lives. In fact, if there was anything in the lives of the kids that could be termed "sacred," music was it. Radios, records, record players were ritual objects of worship, communication totems linking them with their gods: Kiss, The Boomtown Rats, the Bee Gees.

A record collection told where the kid was at. More kids wanted to become rock heroes than firemen, policemen, scientists or, perish the thought, teachers. I asked them what it felt like to listen to their favourite songs.

"Makes me feel free!"

"I feel like me!"

"I forget what's botherin me!"

"I feel like a somebody!"

Because the kids took their music seriously and developed a tenacious loyalty to their individual favourites, fights often broke out over which records to play. Some kids were disco freaks, while others swore by rock 'n' roll. And some kids who liked radio asked for that. I agreed there could be one radio in the class, and told T.J. he could bring in one he claimed to have "found" in an "abandoned" car.

Sal argued that the class would be better off listening to his Elvis Presley collection, but T.J. plugged for his radio. I decided to let the class vote, and called a meeting to debate the issue.

Typically tough in a taut tee-shirt and shades, T.J. opened the meeting by swaggering to the front of the room, hands in his pockets, clearing his throat. "Records are okay, but they got only one or two hit songs in an album. You gotta listen to all the others before you get to the hits. *Nobody* can argue about radio, cause radio plays *all* the hits.

"And another thing," he continued, warming up. "What happens when we go outside in the afternoon? Are we gonna plug a record player into a tree?" That brought a few laughs.

Sal hesitated before speaking, flashing an enraged look at T.J. "Okay smartass!" he said bitterly. "Bring in your dumb radio, but don't be surprised if it gets broke!"

"Here goes another fight," Charleen sighed.

T.J. grinned. "I got my radio right here, man!" Almost magically, he produced a tiny transistor radio, strapped to his wrist. "This is so I don't lose it!" he said to Sal, pointing to the strap.

Sal raised his fist angrily. "Who wants to listen to news? You don't get news on records!"

"News is only five minutes! And you get the hockey scores, too!"

"I hate that ole hockey!" Rhonda bellowed.

"And what about commercials?" Betsy cried.

T.J. jumped on top of his chair, waving his arm angrily. "If you don't want no radio then come and take it!" He stuck out his tongue at Sal.

I stepped in. "Class meetings are for talking things out, not fighting! I'm surprised nobody has suggested taking turns. One day bring in the radio, the next, the record player."

"Good idea!" Charleen exclaimed. "Why not let T.J. bring in his radio Mondays and Tuesdays. Sal and the other kids can bring records on Wednesdays and Thursdays!"

"What about Friday?" Betsy prompted.

"I'll bring my guitar!" Robert chimed in.

T.J. laughed, looked thoughtful, then said, "Deal!"

I rose to my feet. "Meeting adjourned!"

On the way back to my desk, T.J. suddenly turned up his radio full blast. Several kids started to dance. Soon the entire class was moving to the beat.

"Hey sir!" T.J. hollered. "Today's Tuesday! Radio Day!"

How could I forget?

Friday, November 4

I joined a martial arts class to work off some frustration. I go twice a week and work out for several hours. Sometimes I even stay for an extra hour just to punch the bag—the emotional release is great. Martial arts plus the guitar offer me two rather opposite techniques of centering myself emotionally. I recommended them to the rest of the staff.

Wednesday, November 9

Lynn was the bus driver who drove "slow learners" to the school from their homes in the outlying regions. The kids referred to her busload as "Lynn's Loonies."

Lynn was new at the job. Her first request was that the driver's area be enclosed in steel, with a shatterproof glass window directly behind her head for rear viewing.

When that suggestion was turned down, she asked if she could use, instead, a second-hand shark cage. She offered to install it herself if the Board would pay for it.

Nobody appreciated Lynn's sense of humour. She retired after two months.

Wednesday, November 16

John kept slipping books on nutrition into my mailbox. So far, I had resisted his attempts to sell me on the miracles of vitamins, bran and other supplements as just food faddism. Impressed, however, by a number of scientific articles that seemed to back up John's claims, I decided to give it a chance.

I tried vitamins at first and noticed a definite improvement. Then I got into more exotic things like herb teas, ginseng and bee pollen. My friends thought I had flipped, and Jenny and my daughter were threatening to move me out to the garage.

I opened up a health store in the school, run solely by the students themselves. The office gave us a fifty dollar loan, with the understanding that it would be paid back at the end of the year. I stocked up on oranges, apples, bananas, papaya juice, raisins and peanuts. The kids advertised over the public address system.

In the beginning, it caught fire, I had to make emergency trips for new supplies, and we were even thinking of opening up a new line of products.

After a few weeks, the sales dropped drastically.

Apparently the proprietor of the nearby variety store was feeling the pinch, and had begun offering specials on candy to win the kids back. I was stuck with six bushels of apples.

Thursday, November 24

Winter has arrived, so I gave my class an assignment entitled "What I Like To Do in the Winter."

Stash wrote that his favourite event was snuggling into bed at night, pulling the covers tightly over his head, and farting.

Wednesday, November 30

Franko appeared to be one of my better-adjusted students. He rarely got into trouble, was well-liked by the other kids, and showed a keen interest in his subjects. He seemed to be the model student.

Midway through the term, Franko was beaten up by some kids from another class, and shortly afterwards he started to become involved in more fights, sometimes with kids from other classes, sometimes with his fellow classmates. It was puzzling, unsettling—why had a seemingly nonviolent kid turned into a bully, and in such a short time!

When I talked with Franko about it, he replied proudly, "My dad tells me to do it. He's teachin me how to street fight!"

I gave his dad a call, arranging an interview after school. He arrived about four o'clock. When he took his jacket off, I was dazzled: chinos, black boots, a black shirt open to the waist with sleeves rolled up, his powerful arms covered with tattoos: fearless tigers, hearts pierced with arrows, coiled serpents, Canadian flags. His hair was slicked back like a James Dean character, a tiny dark curl resting on his forehead.

He greeted me unsmilingly, shaking my hand firmly. "I'm Franko Senior!"

"Glad you could make it," I replied, rubbing my hand.

"Well, I figure if my son's in trouble, then I should be here, eh?"

His voice was warm and friendly, not nearly as threatening as his appearance. I decided to get to the point right away.

"Franko Junior's been fighting a lot, sometimes without being provoked. I've talked to him and he told me that you told him to fight. That you're teaching him how."

"I didn't know he went lookin for fights," he said, frowning. "But if somebody's pickin on him, that's different. I tell Franko Junior to beat the hell outta him, tell him to get the kind of reputation I had when I was a kid. Nobody wanted to tangle with me, and I'm goin to teach Franko to do the same."

"Frankly," I said, "Franko's not simply protecting himself. He's turned into a bully."

He gritted his teeth: "Hell, if he's turned into a bully, I can fix that! I'll give him a lickin he'll never forget!"

Tuesday, December 13

Betsy had more problems than a ten-year-old should have to cope with. She had an ugly red scar that ran from her lips to her chin—the result of a freak accident on her bicycle. The kids called her "Flip-lip."

While Betsy was in the recovery room, the doctors had tied her into a straitjacket to prevent her from picking at the scab. Her mother felt it was the straitjacket experience that was at the roots of her hyperactivity—one explanation for the way Betsy whirled around my classroom like a miniature tornado.

She and her family lived in a tiny, brown townhouse in the middle of the Jane-Finch high-rise jungle. The family included two older brothers and a German Sheperd named Wolf.

Both her parents had identical debilitating back problems from a near-fatal car crash they had been in several years earlier. Now they spent most of their time stretched out on their sofa or bed.

A constant, gnawing tension ate at the household. The father, now on a meagre disability pension, was unable to work and act his "role" of provider. The mother found equal difficulty in trying to fulfill her "role" as homemaker.

One afternoon Betsy's mother appeared at my classroom door. A tall woman with short, sandy hair, she needed crutches to help her walk. While I dismissed my class for the day she waited.

I had suspected that Betsy was being beaten at home, and her mother admitted it without much prompting. "She seems to be the easiest target, since she's so active, always jumping around and getting in the way all the time," she admitted sadly.

Things became clearer when she told me that she, in turn, was beaten occasionally by her husband. Since the car accident, the family had changed. She agreed to try and control her anger towards Betsy. It was difficult to believe that this animated lady had great difficulty walking across a room, and had spent her whole existence for several years between the bed, sofa and bathroom.

"Doesn't it bother you that your husband beats you, though? Wouldn't it help to work on that end of things?" I asked gently.

"Of course he beats me!" she snapped. "Wouldn't you be upset if you couldn't find work and had to sit home all day doing nothing?"

Soon something came up that gave Betsy a big chance to give her self-respect a boost: the school's talent contest. Any kid could put together an act. She eagerly took a spot in the show.

Somewhere she found a dilapidated banjo. For weeks she practised, but always one simple phrase. Over and over again, she played those same three notes to a perfected monotony; it was too scary for her to try something new.

The evening of the talent show, although I was busy marshalling the kids around, I gave Betsy what support I could. She had arrived an hour early, dressed in a shocking-pink outfit, her hair in tiny ringlets, her lips smeared with lipstick (perhaps to hide her scar). I tried to build up her confidence, but then the sound system blew and Fred insisted I fix it. I didn't see her again until she came on stage— her big chance.

She walked out to the centre stage, looking very confident. I crossed my fingers. Using only a brittle finger, she began to play her single phrase, over and over: "Plunk-a-plunk ... plunk-a-plunk ... plunk-a-plunk...." After about half a minute, the audience became fidgety. Some tried to smile and give her some encouragement, but then I heard from the back what I had dreaded: shouts of "Freak!" and "Flip-lip go home!" Half-pleading, half-demanding that she make a fast exit, the audience called an end to what was to be Betsy's big night. Slowly, more and more people began whistling and stomping and complaining. She stood still, looking confused. At first she actually looked behind her, as if someone else on stage deserved all that abuse. But finally an awful look of recognition came over her face. She knew the audience hated her.

She strode off the stage, gripping her banjo, fighting back tears. She stopped for a moment in the wings, looked out at the jeering audience and stuck out a malevolent tongue.

She missed the next week of school.

Monday, December 5

Mr. McLaren! T.J. punched me in the face!

Fuck off, Flip-lip! Quit lyin!

Look at my nose, sir!

Did you hit her, T.J.?

She pinched her own face—I didn't do nothin! She's tryin to get me!

Come and see my picture on the blackboard, sir!

Did you use paint on the blackboard?

It's okay. It washes off.

I'm not tryin to get him into trouble! He really did hit me!

Will you come up and look at it now, sir?

In a moment.

Is this how you do today's number work?

No ... you were borrowing here. It's an addition question. What do you do in an addition question?

Carry!

Right. You carry, not borrow.

Sir, are you comin up to see my picture?

T.J. just stole my comic books from my desk!

You said you'd help me with my printin, sir.

Just a minute.

I didn't take nothin from Frankie's desk.

I hate printin! Can I just draw instead?

Tell Sal to watch his fuckin welfare face. I'll punch it in for him!

You're welfare!

You're mom's a nigger!

Okay, outside boys! We're going to have a little talk!

My dad used to be welfare sir, but he ain't now. He drives a pickup truck ... he delivers these boxes of flowers.

When are you going to tell T.J. to gimmie back my comic books!

I said for you guys to wait outside!

Garth's dad don't drive a pickup truck, sir. I never seen him drive a pickup truck, and he lives right next door to me.

He gets the truck at work, stupid!

When are you gonna do somethin about T.J., sir?

Who cut the cheese and didn't put out no crackers?

Sal did! I heard him!

It's Betsy!

Come on kids, let's drop the fart questions, okay?

The person that smelled it first is the one who did it!

Then it was Betsy!

You stink, Flip-lip!

Fuck you!

How do you say this word, sir?

Restaurant.

Restr ... ant?

Restaurant. Res ... taur ... ant.

Restrant.

Close enough.

We havin gym this afternoon?

Yes—Monday afternoon as usual.

Can I be captain!

I'm suppose to be captain!

It's my turn!

Sir, come over and look at my paintin.

I asked to be captain first!

We're not having teams today, we're doing gymnastics.

Sir, Sal cut the cheese! This time, I'm sure!

The next time we have teams, can I be captain?

My picture's dry, sir! Will you hurry up or just forget it!

Who said it was me that cut the cheese? Was it you T.J.?
If it was, I'll bash your fuckin head in!

Garth's got a *Playboy* in his desk and he's feeling up the
pictures inside his desk!

What?

Ya, he put his finger up the ass of one of the naked
pictures. There was this picture of a woman bending over
touching her toes.

Garth, can I see you a moment?

Oh, oh.

Sucker!

I got my comic books back, sir, they were in T.J.'s desk,
just like I said.

They're mine! I brought them from home! Honest. My
brother give them to me yesterday!

You asshole! You just wait until I get you outside!

Shut up welfare!

Okay, class. Line up for recess!

Friday, December 16

Christmas reports are nearly due, and the only time I have to
work on them is during lunch period. Since the staff room is
filled with distractions, I took my folder down to the coffee
shop in the local plaza and wrote while I ate.

I had finished and was about to leave when I noticed something familiar about a customer at the front counter.

It was Levon, hunched over a bowl, slouched in his seat exactly as he slouched in his chair when he was in my class. He looked unhealthy, his skin grey and damp with sweat, an ugly cut on his forehead.

"How've you been doing?" I asked, sitting down next to him.

We shook hands. "Hi, McLaren. ... Good to see you. ..." he said. Resting one hand on the counter, he wiped his forehead with the other. Beads of sweat reappeared at once. "Been on bennies these days . . . got to get some sleep. Could you lend me some spare change for another bowl of soup, man?" His voice was weak. He paused frequently, as if out of breath. I reached into my pocket. "Thanks man," he drawled. "I'll pay you back when I'm rich and famous."

Monday, December 19

Sal worked surprisingly hard, considering his well-known abhorrence of math. He was trying. From time to time he looked at me, vulnerable, sad. He whispered to himself. After ten minutes of concentration, his mouth tightened. "I can't do this work no more!" he howled. "I gotta get outta here! I hates my math! I won't do it no more! Nobody forces me to do nothin I don't want to!" he shrieked.

A few moments later, he disappeared out the door. Other kids followed suit.

By the end of the day, I had lost five pupils.

Wednesday, December 21

Rocky is nine. He's a scruffy, wrong-side-of-the-tracks kid with a sincere farmlad face, big square shoulders and extremely large hands. But his head is tiny, and he often grins.

He has the strangest habit of looking at you from an angle that should lead his sight in some other direction. All his movements seem oblique; when he approaches my desk, he never comes directly, but in zig-zags. And he even enters the room sideways, keeping close to the wall so that I always wonder which desk he's making for. Then, at the last moment, he makes a mad dash for his own desk.

Rocky always looks perplexed. He'll raise his hand as if his life depended on it, and then withdraw it as soon as I call on him. A few moments later, he'll be standing in front of me to ask if it's time to go home, usually the first thing in the morning. He'd sooner stare at the ceiling, scribble drawings in notebooks, anything, rather than read. He talks to himself out loud.

He isn't a behaviour problem. The most serious run-in I had with him was when he tricked a group of kindergarten kids into touching the icy, metal fence posts with their tongues. When the kids finally peeled themselves away, they had donated several layers of tongue to the fence.

More than anything else in the world, Rocky wants to join a motorcycle gang. He yearns to be an outlaw biker with full leathers, swastikas and a club crest (his favourite was the Outlaw crest, a skull with two crossed piston rods). He likes the names bikers give themselves: Beast, Mad Dog, Chico, Pig. But the neatest thing about being an outlaw rider, Rocky told me, would be to have a biker funeral, to be ceremoniously carried past rows of shining bikes and be buried in his leather jacket.

Finally, I arranged an interview with Rocky's mother. She looked in her early sixties, too old to have a nine-year-old son. Halfway through our interview she told me she was actually Rocky's grandmother. He was born nine years ago to her fifteen-year-old daughter. Rocky's natural father walked out of the picture before he was even born. The daughter later married and had given birth to two more children before she and her husband filed for a divorce. His grandmother had recently informed Rocky that his older sister was really his mother, and that his nephews were really his half-brothers.

The man Rocky knew as his father (really his grandfather) was on the road to alcoholism and had left the family only months before.

The boy was thoroughly confused. He asked why his real mother had "divorced" him when he was only a baby. He was told how his mother was really too young at the time to look after a baby, so his grandmother and grandfather raised him as if they were his parents.

The grandmother's new boyfriend was waiting outside the classroom while the interview was going on, holding a little baby in his arms. I asked Rocky who the baby was. He told me it was a present from Children's Aid.

Thursday, December 22
I have a full beard. At the class Christmas party, I received twelve bottles of after-shave from my kids.

Monday, January 9
It was Fred who made me more sensitive to the fact that many kids found it oppressive to sit in a tiny classroom, packed with thirty-four other active kids, listening to a teacher bark orders that are not meant to be questioned.

Inner-city kids are restless. By allowing them to discover things for themselves, I found I gave them a legitimate outlet for their excess energy.

I had always divided the morning and afternoon into forty-minute periods, each concentrating on a different subject area. First would come spelling, perhaps, then reading, then math, etc. But now, to give the kids more flexibility and responsibility, I modified this approach. After opening the day, I put the entire day's work on the board. Then I told the kids that they had the rest of the day to cover all the topics, in any order they decided.

They had a great time charting out their timetables. Once they completed the assigned work, they were given free time. Most of them finished about half an hour before the final bell, and spent the free time playing.

As time went on, I kept giving the kids more and more opportunities to generate their own ideas, to choose topics they were especially interested in. It was a slow process, and I had to guide their discussions. But the kids certainly seemed to respond better when given a chance to make some decisions for themselves.

Tuesday, January 10

I asked Sal's mother to come in for an interview. I hadn't counted on the conversation centering on her older son, Jack. "How's he been doing?" I asked, after she had said she was worried about him.

She lowered her head. "Not too good," she said after a pause, mumbling, "he's been in trouble." She lit a cigarette, took a slow drag. "He broke into a house with three other boys. The owner was away for the weekend and the kids heard that he kept guns."

"What happened?" I asked.

"It wasn't my kid's idea, but he went along with it. They really messed up this guy's house—they shit on the floors, and smeared it over the walls. Then they found a little budgie bird in a cage in the kitchen and they tortured it and killed it. Just a little bird. First they cut its wings off with a pair of scissors, then poured boiling water over it, and finally killed it with a blow-torch.

"After nearly wrecking the house, the kids finally found the guns, and they brought them out of the house, wrapped in blankets. And they found bullets, too. They loaded the guns and took them over to the highway and shot them off over the cars."

A look of horror in her eyes and mine. I thought of all the people who use the highway—including myself.

"Did Jack get charged?" I finally asked.

"Yeah. He's got to see his parole officer, once a week."

Now I knew what Sal was referring to when he said his brother was a *big shot* in the neighbourhood.

Wednesday, January 11

T.J.'s mother was redecorating the bathroom with beer bottle labels as wallpaper. She took down an old poster she had hung over the toilet entitled "A Fishermen's Meeting," and told T.J. he could have it for my classroom.

When he brought me the masterpiece, he asked if I would hang it up. I obliged, feeling it would give him a feeling he'd contributed something nice to the room.

The poster read:

Hiyamac
Lobuddy
Binearlong?
Coplour
Cetachanenny?
Goddafew
Kindarthay?
Bassencarp
Ennysizetoom?
Cuplapowns
Hittinhard?
Sordalike
Wahchoozin?
Gobbawurms
Fishanonaboddum?
Rydononaboddum
Whatchadrinkin?
Jugajimbeam
Igodago
Tubad
Seeyaroun
Yeahtakideezy
Guluck

When the parents were invited in to look around the classrooms, one parent looked at T.J.'s poster and said, "Now I know why the kids around here speak the way they do. It's this damn new grammar you're teaching these days!"

Friday, January 20

Every kid carried a comb, but not only for their hair. Combs were weapons. Mostly they were used in threatening gestures. But sometimes a wide swoop connected, leaving a light scar that became a status symbol—it reminded me of the sabre scars once proudly worn by Heidelberg duellists.

At first the black kids had the advantage with the five-pronged picks they used for their Afros. The white kids' standard-issue plastic combs were no match, so they all found nasty long-handled combs to stick menacingly out of their back pockets. A long-handled comb could be used in forward lunges as well as side-swipes.

The most sophisticated comb available looked exactly like a switchblade. You pressed a button on the handle and zap! out shot the comb!

The kids were rarely hurt in their comb warfare. My big worry was that some day a few of them would try out real switchblades.

Wednesday, February 1

By the beginning of February the winter feels like it's dragging on forever. Both kids and teachers are despondent, lethargic. So I decided to boost my class's spirits by offering them an early Valentine's Day gift . . . I booked time at the local ice-skating rink, a whole morning of fun!

A few kids almost froze on the half-mile walk to the rink, since they lacked proper mitts and head-covering, and wore only worn sneakers instead of boots. But somehow every kid managed to scrounge up a pair of skates!

While I was busy tightening some of the laces at one end of the arena, T.J. and a handful of friends sneaked outside to the parking lot. When I went out to investigate, I saw him hacking away at a parked car with his skates, puncturing a tire and punching ugly holes in the body.

I left my name and the school's phone number on a piece of paper and tucked it under the windshield wiper. Then I took the kids back to school. T.J. disappeared along the way.

I was shaking by the time we got back. Here I was trying to do the kids a favour, and I end up worrying about what would happen when the car's owner called!

I waited until four-thirty. There was still no call, so I decided to go home.

As I drove past the school, looking forward to unwinding at home, I glanced up at my classroom window. The kids had already started decorating the window with Valentine's Day messages.

I read the words "I love you, sir" on the cut-out hearts as I slowly drove down the icy road.

Thursday, February 2

John enjoyed eavesdropping at the office, and he picked up an interesting bit of information a few days ago which made me more than a bit apprehensive. One of the Board's consultants would be coming in to visit my class.

"What's he like?" I asked, genuinely worried.

"Well ..." John mumbled, scratching his chin, "he's a good man in many ways, but. ..." I looked at him doubtfully, arching my back to loosen the tight muscles. "Look," he said, running his hand through his hair, "let's say he lives a little in the past ... on the other hand, make it the Stone Age. Know what I mean?"

"Uh ... what exactly *do* you mean?" I wanted to be prepared for the worst.

"Listen ... I'm getting on in years too ... but I've managed to keep up with the times. Let's just say the consultant was arrested, in time, oh, about ten thousand years ago.

"You started out here pretty square. But now you're more like a 'guide on the side,' less like a 'sage on the stage'— say, I like that!" John was fond of corny sayings. "You run a pretty flexible program. You let the kids sit where they feel the most comfortable—he wants to see them in straight rows. You make personal contracts with the kids, and assign work according to what they can handle—he wants to see the same material on everybody's desk. You're physical with your kids, you hug them and so forth—and he wants firm discipline."

I glanced at him uneasily. "I guess he'll destroy me," I sighed wearily.

He shrugged. "Look ... let me give you a suggestion." He put a fatherly arm around my shoulder, and walked me down the corridor. "Go back into your classroom and do everything *just* as you've been doing it. The *kids* like what you're doing, and *that's* the important thing ... not that you're not still a rookie and have lots more to learn." I detected a note of hope in John's voice. "You'll do all right. Tell your kids they'll be having a visitor sometime this month, and promise to give them a reward if they're good."

"Do you really think I ought to do that? Do you think it'll work? I mean, it's bribery, isn't it?"

"I hate to see a good teacher go down the tube," John grinned, waving away my questions like so many flies.

"Any suggestions about what I could give the kids?"

John paused, thinking. "Why not buy them a giant gingerbread house, like in the fairy tales?"

I was beginning to appreciate John more and more.

The next day I discovered a tee-shirt in my mailbox, along with a note. Stencilled across the shirt was: "What— me worry?" The note read: "Good luck, John."

Wednesday, February 8

My class had settled down somewhat. The stress-packed days of experimentation with a variety of programs and approaches was finally paying off. There were still fights, and kids refusing to cooperate, but most of them were getting into better working routines, sometimes teaming up with a partner to investigate items that caught their interest.

In addition to the learning centres, I had set up a drama centre, consisting of a makeshift stage and a box full of old clothes. Kids would act out both their fantasies and their hardships.

Our science centre was a tub of water filled with metric beakers of all sizes and shapes. We also had a mini-library for science, complete with a microscope and several slides (they were of insects the kids collected down by the creek).

But despite the increased response of the kids, I often wondered how much difference any of this would really make in their lives.

Wednesday, February 15

This morning Rod offered to cover my class for the last half hour of the day. I wanted to get an early start downtown to hear a lecturer at the university speak on disadvantaged kids.

I drove several blocks through a heavy snowfall before realizing I'd forgotten my briefcase, so I made a quick stop at the variety store down the road to buy a pen and some paper for taking notes. When I was crossing the street, I heard a couple of "Thanks, man!" I turned to see T.J. and a friend right behind me.

"Where'd you guys come from? Shouldn't you be in school, T.J.?"

"We just came from there," he boasted, "and you gave us a lift." They had bumper-hitched the entire way.

I tried to explain the danger they were courting in

hitching rides that way, but they walked away laughing and threw back: "Different strokes, sir, for different folks!"

Monday, February 20

Bob runs a drop-in centre for adolescents. He's a good friend, and I see him fairly often.

When he began working at the centre, one of his first projects was to get the kids to play floor hockey. The kids insisted that it was impossible because they had no equipment. "Nonsense!" Bob replied, and spent the next few days teaching them how to make hockey sticks out of broom handles, pucks out of wire and cloth, goalposts out of sticks and javex bottles filled with sand, with string for a netting.

With someone to help them, it didn't take any time at all.

Wednesday, February 22

My decision to try to provide my kids with more opportunities for self-direction was unpopular with a few teachers, who regarded with skepticism my attempts to experiment. They pointed to the results of a meeting we had held with some of the neighbourhood parents, who preferred a more authoritarian system. In fact, several parents had complained that I was not using standard readers. Instead, I preferred to create readers out of the kids' own stories.

But, to my surprise, the biggest obstacle to creating a freer attitude in class did not come from the parents. It came from the students themselves.

All their lives they had been ordered to obey rules. They asserted themselves, logically enough, by going out and breaking as many rules as they could. Removing the rules made them uncomfortable; it left them with nothing to push against.

It took months before the kids were comfortable with my policy of having them plan their own timetables, choose their own topics for discussion and reports, and explore their own questions. It also took time for me to free myself of the odd feeling that, because I wasn't following the standard list of teacher topics, I was somehow not actually teaching. . . .

Monday, February 27

Today I talked to an administrator who has done a lot of work with inner-city kids for the Toronto Board of Education. I asked him what his perceptions were about the plight of poor kids in the suburbs.

"I've criss-crossed the entire country and see situations like the one you teach in right across the map. What makes your area a little more frightening than, say, downtown Toronto is that it's so isolated. There are a half-dozen inner-city pockets in the suburbs that are pretty spread out, and there aren't enough social services to help. From the outside the problems are so invisible, they don't get the attention they deserve. At least downtown people know the situations exist, but in the suburbs people try to forget about the problem areas. The scary thing is that there's really an epidemic of instant cities across this country. Yours is just one of many."

That evening I did a lot of guitar playing.

Tuesday, March 7

Renee says her mother doesn't want her bugging her in the house. Her mother always tells her to get lost.

So when she gets home from school, she disappears. From late afternoon until ten o'clock at night, she spends her time quietly reading in the bathtub.

Wednesday, March 8

From the moment Charlie came into Mrs. Rogers' class he made her life miserable. He was so wild, so uncontrollable, that at times she had to resort to pinning him on the floor and calling for help. Once during recess, Charlie tried to settle a dispute with a classmate with a heavy lead pipe. Mrs. Rogers had to wrestle it out of his angry hands. And several times he was caught rifling coats and purses in the teachers' staffroom. He and his newly won followers would come into class late, having lingered in the hallway to urinate in the rows of kindergarten kids' boots.

But Mrs. Rogers didn't give up on Charlie easily. In an attempt to reach him, she tried to befriend him outside the classroom. One weekend she invited Charlie to attend church with her, planning to take him afterwards to a movie and a restaurant. He brought a friend, Tennessee. During the church service they quietly excused themselves and went straight for the cloakroom, where they rifled the coats. They managed to steal enough money to take off for Funland, a popular arcade a few blocks away. Mrs. Rogers found them sitting in a tiny booth, watching a 25¢ strip film.

Without saying a word she drove them back to her apartment, too upset by their behaviour to think about going to a movie or restaurant. When they got to her place, she told them that she wanted to have a frank discussion, and asked them to wait in the living room while she went to the washroom. When she returned a few minutes later she found Charlie and Tennessee giggling together on the floor, a good portion of a bottle of her best Scotch gone.

She kept trying, but over the next few weeks she became completely fed up. After he stole eighty dollars from a secretary's purse, she had him placed on "home study," which meant he had to go to court. The Judge ordered him not to return to school—his education was to be provided by a home tutor. After several months of home study, Charlie's parents had him placed in Thistletown, a hospital for emotionally disturbed youths.

He'd occasionally show up in the school yard to announce to his former classmates that he was going to reform school.

"Hey Charlie!" the kids would say. "Far out!"

Friday, March 10

I constantly had to fight the conditioning I had received in my teacher training and in my first year of teaching. But more and more I was recognizing the incidental questions and conversations of the kids as a learning process. I saw that some of the most effective lessons took place spontaneously: what I often thought was disorder was, in fact, kids interacting in another form of learning.

For example, in the fall T.J. used to bring snakes in from the creek. The kids often crowded around his desk, excited, watching the snake writhe, touching its skin, exclaiming over its colours. It would take me a long time to get them back to their seats and settled down. Thinking about it, I decided that what the kids were learning from T.J. was probably as real as any lesson I could have whipped up.

Freedom, however, is not a magic formula for success. Finding a balance that works requires much patience.

Monday, March 13

She walked into the class with a noticeable limp, her eyes fixed on the floor. Her mouth was a black line; her eyes, which nervously scanned the class, were circled by purple streaks and red gashes; her cheeks were black and blue.

One of the kids whispered to me he had seen her running out of her high-rise building this morning pursued by her mother, who was angrily waving a high-heeled shoe.

When I called her over to my desk, she looked up at me with those sad raccoon-like rings under her eyes with an expression of unmistakable guilt, as if she, herself, had done something wrong. She told me she had fallen off her bicycle.

Tuesday, March 14

One classroom activity that seemed to make the most impact on my group of grade fours involved printing out the phrase "LOVE IS . . ." in big, bold letters on a ten-foot-long sheet of paper. I tacked the paper to the inside of the classroom door. Students could volunteer their reflections on "Love is . . ."

Here's what they wrote:

LOVE IS . . .
A ham sandwich
Christmas presents
When my mom visits Gord in jail
MacDonald's
The Ex
My parents don't fight
When I don't get it for being bad
Being allowed to smoke
Fingering your girlfriend
A honeymoon
Nobody to bug you at night
When your brother goes to dad's place
Fish and chips and vinegar
Going to see dad
Learning to drive
Seeing dad at the restaurant
Smoking grass
Looking after your little brother
Horseback riding at the Y camp
When dad comes over

Thursday, March 16

When Sal arrived in class half an hour late, I knew something was wrong. His eyes, usually clear and bright, were now red and glazed. His face looked blotchy, his hands were trembling.

"What's wrong, Sal?" I asked, giving him a hug, reassuring him I wasn't angry because he was late.

His mouth tightened. "It's ... it's ..." his voice quavered. "It's that dad came home last night, and. . . ."

"What happened?"

Sal stared at the floor, breathing heavily, sniffling loudly. Then he blurted out, "He spent all his pay on lottery tickets, so my mom . . . she gots mad at him cause she needed the money to buy groceries, so I couldn't get no sleep last night cause they was shoutin at each other." He raised his head and stared out the window, avoiding my eyes. "Dad was mad at me this morning, an told me to keep out of his way or he'd bring out the extension cord."

Wednesday, March 29

T.J. arrived in class wearing a black bowling shirt with "Untouchables" stitched in gold thread on the back; he was obviously under the influence—of what, God knows.

He carefully walked to his desk and almost fell into his chair. His mouth was struggling to say something, but the words got stuck somewhere. When he managed to gain some composure, he moved from desk to desk, stammering "Hey you assholes! I'm floatin on air!"

Most of the kids looked a little bewildered, but some of them found it uproariously funny.

"Hey T.J.!" one of the kids shouted. "Got any for me?"

"Come on over to my place after school," T.J. replied. "My mom's new boyfriend's gots lots."

It was hard to tell if T.J. was faking it. A few of the kids enjoyed play-acting at being drunk or stoned; they see it often in their environment. I tried to ignore him and continued with my work.

"What's the matter, McLaren? Don't you ever get stoned?" He began stomping around the room, hair flying, arms flailing. "Go ahead and call the principal, sucker!"

To T.J.'s surprise, I dismissed the class for recess ten minutes early. Then I asked if I could get him some coffee. He couldn't handle being treated nicely. "Sure, McLaren. Big trick, eh? Go get the principal when you go downstairs."

"T.J.," I said, "I'm going downstairs to get you a coffee. If you don't want it, I'll drink it!"

It took me only a few minutes to rush downstairs, grab the coffee and dash back. But by the time I returned, T.J. was gone.

Friday, March 31

Betty had taught in our school for a number of years. Frustrated and bitter, she continually complained about her kids to other teachers.

During lunch, I asked Betty why she hadn't tried transferring from the school—get out into a more middle-class setting. She assured me that the advantages, as far as she was concerned, were all with the inner-city.

"In inner-city communities, parents don't really worry about what kind of program the teachers run, as long as the kid learns how to read and add. It's hard enough getting the parents to meet you for an interview!

"But when you think of it, less involvement means less pressure on you as a teacher. For one thing, you don't have to worry about too many busybody parents trying to run your class like they do in some middle-class schools. A friend of mine teaches in a pretty well-to-do-neighbourhood where the parents are always sticking their noses into the teachers' business: 'Why can't my Johnny do this? Why isn't my Johnny further ahead on that? Blah blah blah!'

"In this school, you don't get that kind of flack. So you put up with Johnny coming to school undernourished. You put up with his misbehaving in class. You put up with the fights at recess. For me, it's a lot better than having the community looking down your throat all the time!"

Few teachers, to be sure, felt the way Betty did. I spoke with many staff members who were proud to work in the inner-city.

If there was a prevailing feeling among the staff, it was of being ignored by the School Board. Most teachers felt an aide for each class was a must, not a luxury. And they felt that the kids newly arrived in Canada needed more "English as second language" teacher specialists, to help them cope.

Monday, April 3

Today the consultant finally paid a visit. I had been nervous about it for weeks, and I took Bill's advice and promised the kids a giant gingerbread house if they behaved themselves.

A dyspeptic old crank who reminded me more of a hawk-faced security guard than an administrator type, he was directed by the Board of Education to go into the classrooms of all new teachers in the area to make sure the teacher knew how to keep the lid on.

One had to question the mentality that found succor in inspecting your cupboards, rating your blackboard script, how neatly you were dressed, how interesting your bulletin boards were and whether they had been changed recently, what kinds of seating arrangements you had, and if the desks were veering off the lines marked on the floor by the edge of the tiles, and whether or not the dates in your daybook were underlined in red ink.

He sat down at the back of the room—a white-haired gentleman wearing a royal blue safari suit with a white belt, with white shoes to match. The desk was much too small for him, but he tried to squeeze in anyway, making him appear ridiculous. He tried to cross his legs, but his knees were too high. I noticed he wore diamond-patterned socks. The more foolish he appeared, the more anxious I became. This man could make or break me.

"I'll be observing you from the back of the room," he had said. "Don't be alarmed if you see me making notes." Butterflies in my stomach. "But carry on as usual," he stated matter-of-factly.

I felt like saying something to break the ice, like: "How do you feel about teaching underpriviledged kids life skills in the first grade?" But the wall of protocol was between us. He would not break it, and I didn't dare.

He stayed at the back of the room, chewing on the rims of his glasses, constantly attending to his little black book even though the lesson hadn't begun. His face alternately went blank and then smiley—I had no idea what his expressions meant. I became terribly paranoid. Had something gone wrong already?

"Interesting bulletin boards," he said in a lugubrious tone, just as the kids came into the room.

What did that mean? Interesting?

I leaned back in my chair, planning ahead to myself, thinking that there shouldn't be any reason why today's lesson would be worse than any other day's. . . .

Nervous, I decided that the reading lesson I had begun would have to be abandoned in favour of something where I could get away with more noise and movement. I sensed the kids were picking up on my uneasiness, and would not be able to contain themselves for long. I was desperate! What could I do?

Gym!

That was it! Gym! I'd take the kids downstairs and play murderball—that way I wouldn't be faulted for having noisy kids. After all, kids were supposed to be noisy in gym! Luckily, there was a free gym period available.

He watched my control as I led the kids downstairs. I was certain he was observing how deftly I could marshall them into line. I imagined his breath on my neck all the way to the gym door. When I turned around at the bottom of the stairs to sneak a glance, I noticed with astonishment that he had disappeared!

All during gym period my nerves were on edge; I figured he would pop in at any moment. The class must have wondered why I was still behaving like an Armed Forces Sergeant with nobody there to watch. And the kids behaved beautifully. No fights, no swearing, no moaning and groaning. They obviously remembered my bribe.

When we returned to the classroom from a picture-perfect half hour of jumping jacks, murderball and relay racing, I was relieved to find he was gone. Apparently, he only intended to visit my room for twenty minutes.

The instant I informed the kids that the visitor had gone, they plugged right back into their more comfortable world of tribal dance, transistor radios and slapstick dances down the halls.

I removed the large brown box from under my desk. Then I sat back and gleefully watched those happy kids devour the gingerbread house in less time than a school of piranha could finish off a roast beef sandwich!

Friday, April 7

Yesterday at lunch hour Fred and I played ping pong. Fred prided himself on his athletic ability and, in fact, was a sensational player. I wasn't bad to begin with and, after playing so much, steadily improved.

I made a bet with Fred in front of the staff. Since I had been a bit late getting to school several times that week, I jokingly told him that if I won the game, I wouldn't have to show up till ten o'clock for a week. If he won, I'd have to arrive a half hour early for a week. Fred instantly took me on, grinning.

After a hard-fought battle, I won the game—and the bet. Of course, it was all a joke, but one teacher thought we had been serious. Today she complained to Fred privately that I was being given preferential treatment. If he didn't break the "agreement" between us, she'd report him to the Federation of Teachers!

Wednesday, April 12

When Laura and I stepped through the front door of her school's "Open House," I realized it was the first time I had been in any other school since I had begun working in the Jane-Finch Corridor; it was like another world. This was definitely not an "under-privileged" area.

The school was beautifully laid out—and no graffiti on the walls! The furniture looked new, and all the classrooms had wall-to-wall carpeting and tiny greenhouses off the balconies where the kids could grow plants.

I couldn't help but fantasize what my class would do to the place if they could switch schools for a day. All the fancy globe lights would be smashed, the greenhouses torn up, the carpets . . . !

I was surprised to see the sophisticated work Laura's teacher had put up on the bulletin boards. This third grade class was doing work that was more advanced academically than what my previous grade six class had been doing. I felt right out of it.

Laura's teacher told me that the only real "incident" in class had occurred when a kid took a pencil from someone's desk and broke it in half. The mother showed up after class with the kid who owned the pencil, complaining about the "permissiveness" of the teacher, since she had allowed such a "terrible" thing to happen!

I went home afterwards and opened a beer, trying to numb the culture shock.

Monday, April 17

Rhonda spent all morning in the library making a cut-and-paste picture of her step-father. She was going to give it to him as a Father's Day gift. When she proudly showed it to the class, however, the reaction was unexpected.

"Ha!" howled T.J. "It looks like a chocolate bar with a bow tie!"

"You know what?" Sal laughed. "If you wet a nigger's lips you can stick em to the wall!"

The class roared. Suddenly T.J. grabbed Rhonda and tried to drag her to the fountain at the back of the room.

"Wet her lips!" Sal cried.

"Stick her to the wall!" other kids screamed.

I rushed over and grabbed T.J., pulling him away from Rhonda, ordering him outside. He took off like a shot and disappeared out the door.

"I don't want to hear the word 'nigger' again!" I told the class sternly. "It's a foul word and hurts people's feelings!"

The class laughed nervously, but they did quiet down.

For a while Rhonda sat at her desk quietly, scribbling all over the picture of her father. Then she finally tore it to shreds. She took out a new blank sheet of paper and began drawing a picture of Darth Vader from *Star Wars* instead.

Tuesday, April 25

For the first time since I came to this school, most of the parents showed up for interviews. Although I had scheduled parents for only fifteen minutes each, sometimes the interviews lasted over an hour.

When they had all left, I saw Fred in the hallway and we walked down to his office for a quiet talk. I told him how depressed I was to find that over half my class came from single-parent families who lived below the poverty line.

Fred cleared his throat, leaning forward. "What we have to do in this school is to accept the child for who he or she is. We can't cloud our minds with the fact that the child comes from a single-parent family, or that the father is a drunk, or that the mother is rarely home.

"As teachers, we can't ignore that, but we can't let it get in our way, either. We have to try to make these kids feel like people—feel like they're worth something. We can't worry ourselves about what to do with a kid who says fuck off, because that's only a symptom of how the kid feels.

"You have to ask yourself if there is any way you can get a child to feel good about himself."

"But what about the racial problem?" I asked.

"Most of the kids from this area don't feel good about

themselves," he replied. "Also, they don't want anybody to feel good as long as they're feeling bad. Misery loves company. So, they pick on the blacks, they pick on you, they pick on me, they pick on the whole damn community because they feel so trapped in their own situation.

"Listen. Teachers have to understand about the prejudices they bring to their job. Somehow, they have to respect the kids' own values, and where the kid is at. We can impose our values on them, but that implies their values aren't any good. That would be destructive. We've got to develop relationships with these kids, and relationships involve feelings, not simply content or information. With poor kids, it's even harder, because you almost have to say to them 'Hey! You're a worthwhile human being, and I don't care where you come from, how you dress, how you look . . . to me, you're great!' " Fred was getting very emotional. His jaw tensed, his arms waved as he spoke, his eyes burning right through me.

"The way you reach a poor kid who's doing lousy at school is not by concentrating on arithmetic, but by getting something going with him or her that tells them that you care about them as people. Forget about the curriculum, at least for the time being. Reach your kids through feelings."

Friday, April 28
I told the kids they could choose any subject they wanted for composition. Here are two I've kept.

If I Could Change Thing in the World

Like no beeting childs
No punching childs
No kicking childs
No hitting childs
No burning childs
No hitting childs with brooms
No pulling childs hair
so nowne sould attak
Ther childs

When kids call other kids nigger or honkey. They are just looking for truble. And if someone calls you a nigger or a honkey it dose not mean have to start a fight. The right thing to do is to pretened that you don't hear what the person is saying. But the other day I had a fight with a girl who called me a nigger and a honkey. And I did the wrong thing. I went and started a fight. And I had a nother fight with a brown girl.

And I told her that me and her are both brown so, if I'm a honkey your a honkey too and if I'm brown your brown too.

Thursday, May 4

At the beginning of the term, Fred hired an American woman named Marsha, who had worked for a year in New York City's Bedford-Stuyvesant area, a rough urban ghetto populated mainly by blacks and Puerto Ricans. She was to replace our Special Education teacher who has resigned, on the verge of a nervous breakdown. Because she had two Masters degrees in Education, the staff quickly looked to her for leadership.

"Listen," Marsha confided to me, after it was obvious that the other teachers wanted her to lead workshops in class management. "I came to Toronto to get away from the problems of teaching in New York! This was the only school that had a vacancy, and that's the only reason I'm here. And from what I've seen so far, you've got some pretty serious problems. Wait about five more years, until the unemployment situation gets worse, and then you'll really be in trouble!"

Marsha was soon making great headway with her kids. We were all pleased with the support and advice she offered us. Her contract, however, was not renewed for the following year because the Immigration Department felt that a Canadian should have the job.

Marsha went back to New York. Rather than return to teaching, she found a job as a legal secretary. We all miss her very much.

Friday, May 12

Jay had greasy hair as black as shoe polish, combed in the style of an early Elvis Presley. He carried his overweight avocado-shaped body clumsily into my room late in the school year.

"I'm the new kid," he said with a nervous smile on his lips. His foot tapped impatiently on the floor while his eyes darted back and forth, up and down ... looking at everything but focussing on nothing. Even his clothes seemed to have a mind of their own. His shirt was half tucked into his pants, his fly unzipped and his shoes undone.

Jay was one of the most hyperactive kids I'd ever seen. For the first few days it took everything I had just to keep him at his desk. When I gave a lesson he'd just fidget around the room, constantly tapping everything and everybody with his ruler.

I decided to phone his mother. As soon as I introduced myself as Jay's teacher, she cut in. "I know ... I know ... he's blasting off again in class! Same thing happened in all his other schools!"

"How many other schools has he attended? I mean, he's only in grade four."

There was a brief silence at the other end of the line. "Six or seven," came the voice again. "Around six or seven other schools."

"Could you tell me why?"

"Well ... these days you gotta take each day as it comes, ya know what I mean? Last month I was all set to move into a house, but my boyfriend moves in with another woman. Before that I was living with a guy who started beating me up. And before that I was kicked out of my apartment because Jay started a fire in the building. Anyway, I'm not budging outa here . . . at least, not right now. My big problem now is Jay. I get so damn desperate with that kid.

"The little brat is always moving or squirming around. Try getting him into bed at night—it's like tucking in a beehive! And clumsy—like a bull in a china shop! I guess you noticed he can't even walk in a straight line. He's always stumbling into his little sister, knocking her down and kicking her in the stomach when she tries to tell him to fu . . . to buzz off. Every night he squirms in front of that damn TV and starts making all sorts of weird sounds; he thinks he's the soundtrack for the shows or something. I mean, he's always yelling and whining and screeching in the background. I get really desperate and sometimes I give him a shot of booze. Damn near got him drunk one night I got so fed up.

"He was on Ritalin cause the doctor said it would calm him down. But somebody told me it could screw up his sex drive when he grows up, so I stopped.

"The real problem was this neighbour I had in the building when he was first born. She's from Jamaica or one of those West Indian Islands where they do all that voodoo and stuff like that. One of the tenants told me to watch out for her—she was a witch or something. I know she put a curse on him. I just know she did!"

Jay's mother went on and on. I decided to let her ventilate, using me as a sounding board. After about half an hour, as she was winding down, I interrupted her long enough to suggest it might be a good idea to send Jay to a food allergist.

As soon as I hung up, I xeroxed her a copy of a diet prescribed by Dr. Ben Feingold, an allergist and pediatrician who maintains that food additives are a major cause of hyperactivity. I don't know if the diet worked, or even if she read it. Three days later she had moved to another neighbourhood.

Wednesday, May 17

Rocky's uncle, a former Black Diamond Rider in the early 1960s, and now a shoe salesman, made up a list for Rocky of all the active motorcycle gangs operating in the country.

All over the cover of his notebook he scribbled the colourful names: Vagabonds—Satan's Choice—Para-Dice Riders—Last Chance—Outlaws—Coffin Wheelers—The Wild Ones—Hell's Angels—The Henchmen—and Gatineau Popeyes.

For once, he spelled everything correctly.

Thursday, May 25

Jewel seemed always to be in a world of her own. She rarely spoke in class, but her creative writing never lacked excitement and richness of expression. Though often quiet and introspective, she always seemed to know what was going on in the outside world. Her stories dealt with adult problems: paying the rent, hassling with apartment superintendents, dealing with welfare officials, finding a decent job, making cheap but nutritious meals, picking up "hot" TVs or transistor radios, or finding ways to earn extra money.

There was a worldliness in Jewel's eyes, perhaps even a touch of smugness, and a supercilious smile rarely left her lips.

Jewel asked me to accompany her home today because some boys who had threatened to beat her up were apparently waiting for her at her building. Asking for help was out of character for Jewel; she was usually so independent. I gave her a drive right to the front door of her building.

When we discovered no suspicious looking boys waiting outside, Jewel just shrugged her shoulders and invited me inside to meet her dad.

After a long ride in an elevator that seemed to stop at every floor, we finally reached her apartment. A sign on her door read: "Cheap Housing Is a Right—Not a Luxury."

Jewel quietly opened the door and led me inside. I immediately tripped over a box of kitty litter in the middle of the living room floor.

Recovering my composure, I paused and looked around. A bird cage with three loudly chirping budgies hung in a corner of the room. Dominating one wall was a large mantlepiece over a false fireplace that held a plastic, plug-in log. Covering the mantlepiece was a glass vase with plastic roses, a tarnished golf trophy, a tiny porcelain zebra, a candle in the shape of a penis and testicles, and a brown earthenware jug that had the words "Brown Jug" painted under the rim. A tattered Mickey Spillaine paperback lay on the floor beside the television. The set was tuned to the Little Rascals, but the sound was turned off. An orange vinyl couch covered in detective magazines and empty TV dinner trays stood only about a foot from the screen. On top of the set was a framed photograph of a young man in a purple tuxedo, purple shirt with black lace trim and a peaked cap. The front of the cap bore the phrase "Do It" in big, block letters.

Jewel noticed me staring at the photograph. "That's my older brother," she said. "He just got married. He sure looks drunk, don't he?"

Beside the photograph stood a lamp with a picture of Niagara Falls painted on the plastic shade. The heat from the light bulb caused some kind of reaction in the shade which gave the appearance of moving water.

"Dad's probably out on the balcony," Jewel said, nudging my arm. "Come on."

She led me onto the balcony where a man was sitting on a lawn chair, buried in a book of detective stories. He looked to be in his mid-forties.

"Hi dad!" Jewel exclaimed. "This is my teacher!"

I stepped across the balcony, ducking under a string of low-hanging patio lights. The man leaned back in his chair, arms dangling, his hair swept and matted up on top of his head like a greasy bird's nest. He looked up at me and extended his hand.

"Yeh. Glad to meet you. I saw you guys pull into the lot. I figured you was Jewel's teacher cause you look like a hippie type. Can I get you a brew?"

"No thanks. Beer hits me pretty hard when I'm tired, and I've had one of those days." I glanced over the balcony and saw the top of my van almost directly underneath. "Boy, you're high up here!"

He reached over, grabbed a plastic lawn chair, and dragged it beside him. "Have a seat here, but be careful. I nicknamed this chair 'the toilet,' so don't fall through."

I noticed that the plastic braiding had been worn through at the centre of the seat, so I sat perched over towards one side. Jewel's dad was grinning. He had a smile like broken glass; his front teeth were chipped and pointed, almost geometrical.

"I didn't know you was comin," he said, removing his book from his lap and placing it gingerly on the floor. "Jewel always wanted me to meet you." He turned his head, blinking at me.

"Well, Jewel's a fine girl and doing well in my class. I brought her home today because she said there were some boys waiting around here to beat her up. I didn't see anyone when we came in."

"Damn kids around here!" he said. "Some of them are okay when you get to know them. But there are the punks!" He spoke with a strange mixture of intensity and detachment, and kept patting his hand through his hair to smooth it back behind his ears, but the oily brown strands kept falling forward again. "There are always the rotten apples," he said, his mouth fixed in a stiff smile.

I glanced down from the balcony again. The sun was beginning to bathe the parking lot in an eerie, sulphur-coloured light. A gang of kids got into a rust-splotched car. The car screeched away, leaving a cloud of blue smoke that lingered in the lot long after the car had disappeared.

"Damn kids!" Jewel's dad remarked bitterly. "Ain't they ever heard of noise pollution?" He took a pipe out of his vest pocket and clenched it, unlit, between his teeth. He sucked hard several times. "I feel sorry for all the riff raff you gotta teach in your class. If I were a teacher today, I'd carry a gun."

Jewel, who was sitting quietly in the corner, jumped up. "Daddy! Would you want Mr. McLaren to shoot me?"

Her father swung around in his chair. "Not you sweetheart! Just the punks!" He turned around slowly and faced me again. There was a sad expression in his eyes. "I sometimes wonder what's happenin in the world. I don't want Jewel mixed up with a lot of these kids. I was just readin a story about two thirteen-year-old hit men charged with the killin of a numbers racketeer in New York. It's a true story. Some crook gave the kids a loaded 20-gauge shotgun. And I just read that a coupla teenagers set a wino on fire for kicks. The mother of one of the kids is mad because her son is going to jail for killin a bum. And here, in this country, this teenage girl threw herself off a balcony—only a mile or so from here. This guy finds the body, drags it behind the buildin, and rapes it like a piece of cold meat. I think the guy was from South America. They sent him back home." He paused. "Tell me Mr. McLaren, do you believe in castratin rapists? I do!"

I stared at the floor. My head was swimming. I didn't know what to say. "Life is hard. Nobody has to tell you that. We live in troubled times. I don't know what's happening in the world. I'm just as confused being a teacher as you are as a parent. Somehow we've got to carry on—teachers and parents—and not give up and even work together."

Jewel's dad sucked again on his unlit pipe. His jaw began to tighten and his aquiline nose gave his expression a certain animal quality. "Jewel likes you. At first I wanted her to have a woman teacher cause her mother walked out on us last year. Maybe now I should feel lucky she has you. You know, I just pray I can go through life without anythin happening to Jewel. I mean . . . I mean I really worry about her. She's all I got and I'm all she's got. If anything ever happens to her I think I'll throw in the towel for keeps."

Monday, May 29

I told Marta that she couldn't go to the library before the other kids; she had to wait her turn. She grabbed the stapler out of my desk, and before I could stop her, she had fired three staples into her thumb.

Wednesday, May 31

It was a professional development day at Laura's school today, so I decided to bring her along with me. Even though she was a year younger than my kids, she was looking forward to meeting them and seeing my classroom.

When I pulled into the parking lot, T.J. and Sal ran up to my van. "Who's that?" they asked.

"I'd like you to meet my daughter, Laura."

"I didn't know you had a kid," T.J. laughed. "Hiya, Laura. I'm the leader of the class, and I own all the kids in the room. They do what I tell them to."

Laura smiled as we made our way through the crowd of kids towards my room, Sal and T.J. following close behind.

"Hey, Laura," T.J. snickered. "You gotta nice ass."

"Easy does it, T.J.," I cautioned, "I want her to have a nice day."

Once inside, Laura took a seat next to my desk. The kids poured into the room, giggling and pointing at her. She just stared at the floor, feeling very embarrassed. Halfway through the morning art lesson, Betsy began shifting uneasily in her chair. Then she started to groan softly, smoothing her hands down her legs. "Oh, sir," she whispered, licking her lips slowly and sensuously, "you really turn me on." Her hands started to cup her underdeveloped breasts. "I wish I had X-ray glasses on so I could see your balls."

My face grew red. "Step outside the room, Betsy."

Laura continued staring at the floor. I picked up a yardstick, gripped it tightly, and started tapping the back of my chair.

Suddenly T.J. stood up. "Hey sir, can I go outside with Betsy?"

"Stay where you are!"

"But you got her mad!"

"She deserves to feel mad."

"Why're ya hasslin her just cause she's got the hots for ya?"

"Okay, T.J. Change the subject. Everybody take out your math notebooks—we're going to have a little drill."

When the recess bell rang, I took Laura over to the main building, where the caretaker played ping pong with her for the rest of the morning. During the afternoon she helped Marge, the librarian, arrange books.

On our trip home she noticed something in her coat pocket—a crude drawing that depicted me having sex with a voluptuous woman.

After that, Laura never wanted to come back to the school.

Friday, June 2

T.J. enjoyed staying in the room at recess to fiddle with parts from a car engine that I had brought in for the class. When I wasn't on yard duty, I'd often join him. I tried initiating conversations with him, with the idea that he needed somebody to talk to about his troubles, an adult who would actually listen.

When we talked, T.J. would doodle in his notebook. We started off slowly, so I wouldn't scare him off. At first, he doodled pictures of souped-up racing cars. He designed a special car that appeared in many of his drawings: the "Death Machine," as he called it. Later on, he drew other things . . . whatever came into his mind. Sometimes, when he was feeling burnt-around-the-edges because of events at home, he'd illustrate some unpleasant episode centering around his family.

I showed his pictures to a friend of mine who was a

trained art therapist. He told me that whoever drew those pictures was a very sick boy ... possibly with alarming tendencies. But an art therapist can never know for sure until he interviews the child over a period of time.

Since it was almost impossible to talk to T.J.'s mother at her house because of all the commotion, I tried to convince her to come to see me after school. I told her I wanted to try and improve their "channels of communication" with each other.

"We're *communicating* just fine!" she told me over the phone. "He gets my message! When I tell him to do something, he does it, or else! And he knows what the 'or else' means!"

She also said that she didn't believe in all that "psychology bullshit." "If *I've* never had it, and *I've* made it this far, why can't T.J.?"

Thursday, June 8

Teresa hated going home after school. She didn't ask me if she could stay after class because she liked school; she wanted to avoid the gang of boys who waited outside for their "collection."

The gang demanded different things from different kids. Willy was told to bring coins, Tracy comic books, and Teresa was to steal gum from the variety store at the plaza. Punishment for not coming through with the goods was a beating. No matter how carefully the teachers tried to prevent it, we simply couldn't be everywhere at once.

So Teresa's mother went to the store each week and bought bags full of gum for the gang members—she didn't want her daughter to have to steal.

Saturday, June 10

I decided to bring groups of kids home to my tiny bungalow in the Beaches district. We could walk down to the lake and explore the beach, stroll along the boardwalk, or skip stones in the water. Over four Saturdays, I planned to entertain the entire class.

Jenny relished the idea of playing the good fairy. She spent hours dreaming up games and activities, and even more time overspending our budget, gathering an assortment of food that included oyster soup, lasagne, quiche lorraine and shrimp.

This afternoon at the beach the kids dashed about like little madcaps. They gathered odd bits of glass and stone, played games of tag and British bulldog and sunbathed near the water. Some kids boogied to blaring transistor radios, while others postured for my movie camera, much to the delight of the people strolling along the boardwalk.

The day went beautifully ... until we decided to try having a campfire. Immediately, Sal and T.J. started fighting over who would light the fire. I saw T.J. angrily throw a rock at Sal, watching helplessly as the rock sped through the air and narrowly missed his head. He collapsed in a half-faint. First I made sure he was okay, then I calmed T.J. down. No one had actually been hurt.

Later, I found the rock T.J. had thrown, a pretty big one. When I picked it up, I could barely manage to heave it any distance. His anger must have generated a great burst of strength. No wonder he won so many fights.

Dinner was a big success.

At the end of the day, my wife made her farewells to the kids. She didn't understand that street kids don't say any words of thanks. Because they have so little, they feel they deserve whatever they can get.

"Did you kids have a good time?" she asked brightly, as they were getting into the van for the trip home.

One kid said, "Well, it was all right, I guess. . . ."

Another chimed in, "We shoulda gone to Ontario Place!"

"Na!" T.J. jeered. "Who needs this, anyway? I have more fun at my place, just hangin aroun!"

Monday, June 12

Today I bumped into Brian, a lad I had taught in my first year teaching in a middle-class school. He had been one student that I was sure was destined for good things—a textbook paradigm of a writer-to-be. At thirteen he was composing prolific verse which was incredibly sensitive, insightful and wonderfully rhythmical for a boy his age.

He now loomed before me, over six feet tall, wearing a checked peaked cap, fatigue jacket over a goose-down vest, and worn Kodiak boots. His face, formerly soft and placid, had grown tight and severe. He looked as hard as a clenched fist.

"Hey McLaren, how ya doin?" he asked huskily, taking my hand in a vise grip and shaking it vigorously. "Are you still teachin?"

"I sure am," I replied. "Tell me, how's that wonderful writing of yours coming along?"

A profound sigh. "I gave that shit up last year. I gotta girlfriend now, though. She likes to dance so I'm into dancin now. We go to this disco joint most nights."

"I never would have taken you for a disco freak," I smiled. "How's your schoolwork coming along? Still at the top of the class?"

Brian's face twitched slightly and he nervously began playing with the peak of his cap. "I quit school last year," he said defiantly. "I'm over sixteen."

"Oh."

"Ya ... well ... I'm learning to lay foundations for cottages now. So if you ever want to build a cottage, you know who to call. But I've nearly decided to split that scene and move down here. Damn mosquitoes up north this time of year are big enough to fuck hens!"

"Not exactly a poetic metaphor," I chuckled.

Brian smiled widely, revealing two missing front teeth, partly camouflaged by a flimsy moustache. "If I'm still up there this winter, why don't you gimmie a holler and come up for a ride on my cat?"

"Your cat?"

"Ya—you know—Arctic Cat. I'm really heavy into snowmobiles."

He scribbled his address and phone number down on a piece of paper and pushed it into my hand. "See ya later, sir! Don't do anythin I wouldn't do and if ya do, name it after me!"

Thursday, June 15

I was interrupted in class by a cry of "Sir! Sir! Your shoe!" Since it was raining heavily outside, my first thought was that my shoes were muddy, and I had trekked dirt into the classroom.

But when I looked down at my crossed legs, I was astonished to see one of my pupils, new to the school, vigorously licking the underside of my shoe.

I jerked my foot away. When I turned the shoe over, I saw a large patch on the sole had been licked shiny clean.

Tuesday, June 20

As an end-of-year treat, I took the kids to the Metro Zoo. They were totally high on the idea.

At first things went well, but problems arose almost as soon as the tour guide opened her mouth: "Now, boys and girls, let's find out as much as we can about these strange and wonderful creatures, shall we?" she minced, smiling sweetly.

"Do you mean T.J.?" Betsy quipped.

At once, the tour guide became ticked off. She tried to draw the kids' attention to the tapir and its snout, but the kids rapidly drowned her out with cries of: "What's a snout?," "Who cares?," and "I wanna see the gorillas!"

The tour guide's lines were too well rehearsed, with a slogan-like rigidity my kids couldn't handle: "This is a peacock, look at its pretty tail!," or "Look at all the wrinkles on

the elephant . . . doesn't it remind you of your grandfather?"
I didn't have the heart to tell her most of the kids had no idea
who their grandparents were.

The kids soon found her an annoyance, and wanted her
to get lost. I decided I'd better take them around on my own.

To placate the zoo's security staff, who were beginning
to give us rueful looks, I marshalled the kids into a sem-
blance of order, and off we went.

The Metro Toronto Zoo's plan for keeping the animals
separated from the human visitors involves a series of dry
moats instead of the usual pens and steel cages, though in
some places there were fibre-glass shields. It was possible to
leap across the moats, if you were crazy enough to want to.
Naturally, that's just what some of my kids wanted to do. It
didn't seem to matter if the animals were hippos, rhinos or
giraffes. The kids wanted to shake hands—though I noticed
they didn't try anything with the lions.

At the pink flamingo exhibit, T.J. thought it would be
hilarious to see if he could throw a stone and snap the bird's
spindly leg. "Its leg is so skinny I could break it with my little
finger," he boasted.

At the gorilla exhibit, he pointed to one of the West
Indian kids, remarking: "Hey, Winston! There's your mom
and dad! Jump in, and let em wipe your ass!"

Next to the gorillas and Egyptian fruit bats (which, to
the kids' delight, defecated upside down), the kids thought
the very best part of the trip was . . .

. . . was MacDonald's restaurant.

Friday, June 30

I threw a class party, and it went very well. Afterwards,
Muscle Lady dropped by to wish me happy summer holidays. Her tee-shirt read: "Four out of five dentists recom-
mend oral sex." I asked her how my former students were
doing. "Same as always," was the reply. "We ain't changed a
bit."

On my way out I met a visiting teacher from the nearby junior-high. "You taught Buddy in grade six, didn't you?" he asked.

"Not officially, but I spent a great deal of time with him. How did he make out this year?"

"He's a real behaviour problem. But last week he ran into some problems outside the school, too."

"Problems?"

"Yeh," the teacher continued, "he was rushed to York-Finch Hospital on the weekend."

"No kidding. What for?"

"He got stuck to a dog—sexually, if you know what I mean. It took the intern in the emergency ward to get them apart."

Epilogue

During the last week of school, I asked Fred to reserve a position in the primary grades for me, just in case somebody decided to resign or transfer during the summer. He told me there was a vacancy in grades two-three; I could have it if I wanted it. Well, I told him I was still searching for my "right" grade level and was happy to take the offer.

Fred was glad to have a male teacher in the lower grades. He felt that kids should be exposed to male authority figures as early as possible. Many of the kids at the school, he felt, needed male teachers because they didn't have any permanent father figures at home.

Teachers make a ritual of getting together at the end of the year to discuss who would be getting this year's kids next year. Sometimes a big fuss was made when a teacher knew he was getting a kid who was a real problem. Teachers trying to avoid having a certain kid placed in their classroom might say their program "wasn't appropriate," or that their classroom wasn't designed to "accommodate excess motion." Staff members would even trade certain kids for others; it was a real marketplace.

T.J.'s little brother, Mickey, ended up on my list; Mickey's grade two teacher thought I was the right person for him. She had observed my program, liked what I was doing, and decided that a freer atmosphere would be the best thing for him. At first, I didn't mind. But then I began to feel apprehensive. I remembered some of what I had just gone through with T.J., and every day Mickey was getting to be more like him.

I remembered that first time I saw him—when I had gone to T.J.'s for lunch and saw Mickey running and swearing after a police cruiser carting one of his brothers away. I knew what I'd be in for if he ended up in my class.

I was a little resentful of always being given the "hard cases." Male teachers were usually given the wildest and most disorderly students because they were better able to physically defend themselves. I didn't mind taking my share of disorderly kids, but I felt that some teachers sent me certain kids to relieve other teachers who were their pals. It was a con game using the kids as dice, and like any other con, it stunk.

Still, in the end, I took Mickey on.

"What kind of a plan do you have for him?" Rod asked when he'd heard that I'd finally agreed to take on a student no one else wanted.

"What Fred always prescribes. Tender loving care," I replied, somewhat sanctimoniously.

I had learned a fair bit and had made it through another year, doing my best to care for the kids in a loving way, and still keep their respect as a teacher. I knew I couldn't become "one of the gang" because kids have their own pals and certainly don't want their teacher to be one. But I felt they were starting to respect me more because they knew I cared about them, and at the same time they knew I had certain expectations of them. I ran a pretty tight, but flexible, ship. I tried to provide security and structure, and the freedom, I hoped, to explore and discover.

Now that I had a permanent teaching certificate, my career seemed set. The problem was—could I remain happy as a teacher for the rest of my life? I was having misgivings about emotionally surviving these kids for the next twenty or thirty years. I wasn't the administrator type and had no intention of going the vice-principal route that so many male teachers in the system long for; so many of them get trapped by security—but it's understandable. My mortgage payments looming every month tamped down my growing feelings of frustration. But I promised myself that once I felt that I wasn't offering a hundred per cent to my kids, I'd pack it in.

Jenny and I had been planning all spring to celebrate my new status with a trip to Cape Cod, and two days into the holidays our van was packed and off we went. Most afternoons we spent just sitting in the sun, relaxing and reading. Whenever Laura and Jenny were in Hyannis doing some shopping, I sat by the ocean and worked on a series of poems. And however much I consciously tried to "turn off," the themes invariably turned to my kids and the classroom. I started brooding about returning to the classroom.

<pre>
corridor kids
   from dead end shores
what thoughts possess you?
   those old streetwise eyes
set in smooth
        young heads
  stare blankly
        at a teflon dreamscape
sear through memories
  of innocence on the rampage
corridor kids
  the past
        frozen like smoke
  in a photograph
        dissolves sulphur sweet
into tomorrow
</pre>

Once we got back to Toronto, I searched my basement for primary curriculum guidelines and activities I had stored away since Teacher's College. I also phoned some of the primary teachers at the school and asked them to round up any interesting books, resource material or lessons that would help me.

I saw T.J. towards the end of the summer vacation when I went back to the school to prepare my classroom for September. As I drove into the school parking lot, I noticed a wry-necked figure hunched over a skateboard. He was crouching on the curb, trying to fasten together the broken laces of his Kodiak boots. I smiled at him, but he didn't smile back.

"I came back to visit," he said dryly, balancing on the tip of his skateboard with admirable skill.

"Visit?"

"Didn't ya know? We got kicked out." He spoke quietly. "Ontario Housing kicked us out . . . we didn't have the bread."

"Where are you living now?"

"In the zoo, a couple of blocks over."

"How do you like it there?"

"It's the pits. The cops there are real turkeys. I got charged with assault, man. Can you believe it! This cop said I punched this kid out, but I didn't, so I clobbered the cop over the head with a stick. He tried to put the cuffs on me, but I didn't let him." He started riding his skateboard in little circles. "Can I still come and see ya?"

"Of course, you're welcome any time."

"See ya," he said, waving goodbye. "I gotta look up a few kids—got some unfinished bizness."

"The Suburbs Was Supposed To Be a Nice Place . . ."

3

Tuesday, September 5

It was a great convenience keeping the same room. I was spared the job of moving all my paraphernalia; the bulletin boards didn't even need changing. During the summer the caretaker had replaced all the desks and chairs with smaller versions to accommodate the younger kids. I was ready!

As the kids began hurrying through the door, I was amazed at how tiny they were. I felt like a giant shambling among a room full of elves.

"He's the first man teacher I ever had!" I overheard one kid say. "If he's like my step-dad, I'm gettin outta here!"

Friday, September 8

"Does anybody know what the hardest part of the body is?" I asked the class during a science lesson.

"The head!" "Feet!" "My chin!" "Knees!" "Back!" "A fist!"

Finally a kid called out: "Teeth!"

"Right you are!" I exclaimed. "Now, does anybody know what teeth are made out of?"

"Stones!" "Cement!" "Bones!" "Shells!" "Plastic!"

"It's called enamel," I told them, "and it's the hardest substance in the body."

At which Mickey shot up his hand at once, yelling, "If it's the hardest part of the body, then how come I broke a guy's front teeth with my fist?"

Monday, September 11

I decided to work on Fred's philosophy of improving the child's self-image—a difficult undertaking sometimes, trying to show love for a child who is driving you crazy. But the method had worked fairly well for me with T.J., and I was confident that Fred's approach would be even more effective with the younger kids; they would be less hardened and would find it a little easier to accept a teacher as someone who actually cared about them.

I looked forward to hugging the kids and giving them the support they needed, while not having to endure the resistance the older kids showed.

At first, I organized programs for the kids in role-playing, psychodrama, as well as other activities geared to improve their self-image. Later on, I had to abandon the idea of working with the class as a whole, simply because the kids really didn't have the required social skills to do activities in a large group. There was too much pushing, shoving, swearing and fighting.

Smaller groups proved more effective. Some of the kids responded by calling me "daddy," and a few of them asked me if I'd marry their mothers. But, as usual, there just wasn't enough time in the day to give each child the care and attention he or she deserved.

The myth I held that older kids were probably neglected because they could fend for themselves was destroyed. Many of my seven- and eight-year-olds were just as messed up; their lives were equally sad.

Tuesday, September 19

Samantha and Priscilla were talking at my desk.

"I'm glad I'm black, aren't you?" Samantha asked her friend.

"Yah," Priscilla replied. "Black is beautiful. My mom keeps tellin me that, over and over."

"We're brown now cause we're small. But when we gets older, we'll turn dark black."

"Yah. I wish sir was black, don't you? Mr. McLaren, will you be black?"

"How am I supposed to do that?" I asked.

"My mom says that if you're brown, you can go to the hospital and they make you white. If you're white, you can come out black. You gots to have an operation, though."

"If you're a girl and wanna be a boy," Samantha added, "you can gets the doctor to make you a boy."

"I don't wanna be no boy," Priscilla protested.

"Me neither! My mother had a sister friend, you know, who don't wants to be black. So she had a sex operation and came out white."

Thursday, September 21

Mickey worshipped his older brother, T.J. He acted as part sidekick, part slave, following T.J. wherever he went. He scurried down the halls ahead of T.J. just to open doors for him.

At the beginning of the term, T.J. dropped by my room to voice his approval at Mickey's being in my classroom. "Keep him outta trouble," he warned me, grinning.

"I'll do my best, T.J."

"If he gets outta hand, just call on me, man. I'll come down and smack him silly!"

Friday, September 22

I went for a walk to the nearby variety store after school. It had been raining and the streets were glistening wet. I made my way past rows of neat bungalows with hedges and bedraggled petunias. There were lots of dogs, including several ferocious-looking Dobermans on chain leashes sitting in the front yards, waiting for a passer-by to bark at.

The variety store was located in a tiny plaza, comprising a milk store, variety store, fish-and-chip shop and a women's hairdressing salon. Scribbled over a long-faded sign was the warning: "Keep Out! Property of the Dukes!" Crowds of kids filled the streets and sidewalks, which were littered with refuse.

To prevent break-ins the variety store was covered by a protective wire mesh. One kid was trying to scale it like a human fly, but his feet were too big to gain a secure footing and he soon gave up. Outside the store several boys stood spitting into rain puddles which filled the holes in the sidewalk. Two teenagers in overalls slumped against the wall, uncorked a bottle of cheap wine and took several quick swallows. The empty bottle was tossed down a mud slope to the street below, where it smashed into pieces and woke up a toddler sleeping nearby, who started to cry. Children sat on the slope, watching the street and drawing figures in the dirt with their bare toes, while two laughing kids somersaulted down, somehow managing to stop themselves before they tumbled into the traffic.

I saw two girls from my class sitting on the curb across the street, smoking. One waved her hand while the other frowned and flicked her cigarette in my direction.

I bought some pipe tobacco in the store and watched while the store manager threatened some kids with a sawed-off broom handle. Then I headed back to the school, wondering what I could teach the following day that would really grab these kids.

Monday, September 25

Victor had a problem. He was always pulling his pants down in front of other kids—and he was encouraging them to do the same. His mother beat him for it, to no avail.

Once, in class, Victor swaggered up to Mickey, unzipped his fly, and stuck a glue bottle inside. Then while Mickey stood there startled, just staring at him, Victor wiggled the glue bottle up and down, chanting: "Mickey's got a sticky cock! Mickey's got a sticky cock!"

Mickey slugged him.

Victor did it again and, before I could do anything, Mickey hit him again.

This week Victor was enrolled in a clinic for emotionally disturbed kids.

Thursday, September 28

Anna and Suzanne asked if they could clean the classroom up during recess.

"We promise to make it look great, sir!"

"Wait till you see it, sir!"

When I returned after recess, I found that the desks were covered with fresh magic marker swipes and obscene graffiti. "Moosecock" was scribbled across the map of Canada. The ribbon on my typewriter was in shreds in the sink, with inky blue water spilled all over the floor.

Kids complained that their lunches were missing and one girl couldn't find her glasses. I noticed the window facing the street was open and looked outside to see books, papers, lunch pails and glasses scattered on the ground.

I kept Anna and Suzanne in after school to clean up the mess, but needless to say, after that I did without recess helpers for a while.

Thursday, October 5

Tracy now wears a brace.

Late one afternoon, she tried to imitate Evel Knievel's jump over the Snake Canyon, her version a make-shift wooden ramp in back of the local Miracle Mart. She had even less luck than Evel: she broke her back.

Her elaborate brace thrilled and inspired the other kids when she returned to class. They'd seen "The Bionic Woman" on TV, and decided to find out if Tracy was bionic too. They left tacks on her chair to see if she felt pain; they poked her in the legs with pencils to see if she would short-circuit. And not a few asked her to jump up to the school roof with her bionic legs to retrieve their lost balls.

Wednesday, October 11

Charlotte taught perceptually handicapped students. I got to know her when she asked to integrate her kids occasionally into a regular class setting for part of the day, and asked if we could combine our two classes. I agreed enthusiastically.

She owned a giant Great Pyrenees dog, Pip, which she brought to school each day. Usually that's an impossibility, since there're always kids who suffer allergies. But so far there hasn't been a single complaint. Everybody loves Pip; he's a great, big, lovable shmoe.

One of Charlotte's kids—Bruce—took a special liking to Pip. He soon became obsessive about being next to the dog, developing a wild possessiveness that scared the rest of the class away. Bruce is a big kid. One day he attacked several kids just because they fed Pip some scraps from their lunch boxes.

Charlotte had to find out more about him, so she got in touch with Bruce's father. His parents were separated and the father had custody of Bruce, while the mother kept his two brothers. Bruce had had his own dog that he desperately wanted to take with him when he left. But his father had moved into a building where dogs weren't allowed, so the dog remained at his mother's house.

After Bruce left, his two brothers had stoned the dog to death.

Friday, October 13

Today Mickey turned to me, smiling, and said, "Watch this, Mr. McLaren!"

Then he hit himself against his forehead with the steel edge of his ruler: whap! whap! whap! Deep red welts rose up over his eyes. He continued to smile, as if nothing had happened.

Tuesday, October 17

Samantha was staring at me, clearly full of anger.

"Something wrong?" I asked her, walking up to her desk.

She put her hands on her hips, hissing: "Your face looks sickly pale today. You needs a suntan!"

I frowned. "Do I look pale? I feel fine!"

"She means you're a whitey!" Sue snapped, also angry.

"Samantha's mad at you today!" Priscilla, sitting on the other side, barked.

"Is that true?" I asked. "Are you mad at me Samantha? If you are, let's talk about it."

Snorting at my suggestion, Samantha instead got up and walked slowly to the reading centre, her face full of exasperation and suspicion, Sue and Priscilla following. The three girls had grown up together in Jamaica and were fast friends.

I followed them over. "Samantha, are you going to tell me what's bothering you?"

There was a profound hurt in her eyes. "Why do white people always fire black people from their jobs?" She used a tone of voice I'd never heard her use before.

Her question caught me by surprise. "What do you mean?"

"My dad gots fired from his work yesterday. He told me whitey likes to fire black people. Is that true?"

"Well," I said, swallowing hard, "sometimes there is prejudice, but—"

"Last year we had a black teacher! Now she's gone!" Sue spat out. "We gots lots of black kids in this school. How come we don't gots more black teachers? How come Mrs. Jones was fired and not some white teacher?"

"Yah," Priscilla chimed in. "And how come the people who do all the firing's always white?"

I explained that the Board had fired all teachers who had the least experience, because of budget cutbacks. "Honest, Samantha, Mrs. Jones wasn't fired because she was black." But my voice lacked conviction.

A pause.

Samantha's brow raised in a curious puzzled expression. "I told my dad *you* don't lie, sir. So I guess I believes you. But you know what my dad said?" Her eyes softened and her mouth relaxed.

"What?"

"He said if you don't lie, you must be the only honkey that don't." She grinned.

I laughed and the girls laughed.

Inside, I felt like crying.

Friday, October 20

Mickey picked his nose and ate the snot. When I was a kid, my best friend was a snot-eater.

Sometimes several nose-pickers would have "snot wars," and often their assignments reflected the results of these battles in the form of little green boogies caked to the paper. Snot wars were not popular, but they did exist.

Snot-competition was more commonplace, although it was not the sort of thing you would see every day. Kids would compete for the longest piece of snot, dangling their finds on the ends of a raised finger tip.

Monday, October 23

A rummy lived in the park behind the school. Kids spotted him picking through junk and putting choice items in a duffle bag he kept beneath the sewer pipe he called home. They were fascinated with his wizened old face festooned with coarse, scarlet patches. His lank, black hair was long and greasy.

Some kids claimed Rummy exposed himself to small kids who came across his hideaway. Then again, Rummy was accused of everything from mutilation to murder. I got a lot of mileage out of Rummy in the kid's creative writing assignments.

If a kid lost something on the way to school, Rummy had it. If there was a family fight, Rummy caused it. If a kid was mysteriously absent from class, Rummy had captured him on the way to school and was in the process of devouring him raw. The kids had found someone to blame for all the problems in their universe.

Now that Rummy has moved out, they continue to use him as a scapegoat, sort of by long distance.

Tuesday, October 24

"Okay kids!" I started off the geography lesson. "What's the capital of Canada?"

The answers came, thick and fast:

"George Washington!"

"Captain Kangaroo!"

"Canada!"

"No, no," I told them firmly. "I'm asking for the capital city of Canada. A city, not a person."

Silence. Then Mickey stood up, stared at me quizzically, then shouted: "Mexico!"

Suddenly, half the class was shouting: "Florida!" "China!" "Marineland!" "City Hall!"

"Listen," I said patiently, "if you just all settle down a bit, I'll tell you the name of the capital of Canada. Okay?"

"Don't tell us, sir!" Mickey blurted. "I know the answer!"

"Okay, Mickey," I said. "One last try."

He took a deep breath. "Guy Lafleur!"

Friday, October 27

"My dad's gettin a new van," Jessie proudly told the class.

"Great," I prompted. "What kind?"

"I don't know, sir. But you know what, sir? It's gonna have a bar, and a bed, and lots of pictures of girls, naked girls, with big tits stickin out and tips on them like bottle caps, Mr. McLaren! From magazines! Me and my brother gots a bunch we ripped out for the walls," he smirked wickedly, "and we gots to get some more for the ceilin!"

I felt myself beginning to blush. Teachers aren't supposed to blush; we're always supposed to be in control. So I cleared my throat and tried to nip this in the bud. "What's your brother and a seven-year-old kid like you going to do with a van like that? And those naked girls. What do your mom and dad think?"

"Well, I can't drive yet. But my mom and dad says my brother can use it to screw his girlfrien in, but they has to have it for campin in the summer."

Monday, October 30

Megan is a quiet, almost invisible child. She always stands alone at recess, almost motionless, except for fondling her lank hair. She hardly ever speaks, never gets into trouble, always completes her assignments, never interrupts a lesson or shows up late for class. I like her, but usually I hardly know she is there.

This afternoon the secretary left a message for me to call Mrs. Llewellyn. Who was Mrs. Llewellyn? When I returned the call, Mrs. Llewellyn turned out to be Megan's mother, and she was angry: "Now listen Mr. McLaren! I'm getting ready these psychiatrist papers on Megan! Tell me this! Does she daydream in class?"

"Megan? What's wrong?"

"How do I know! I just know I'm fed up with her! Fed up! I've got a nitwit for a daughter!"

I was able to calm Mrs. Llewellyn down and promised

to have a closer look at Megan. Apparently she never talks at home, either, and spends most of her time alone in her room.

From now on, I'll try to pay more attention to the quiet Megans in my class.

Thursday, November 2

When Gracie threw a heavy glue bottle at Pasquale, I called her mother in for an interview.

Gracie's dark-rimmed brown eyes and spiked lashes and her long platinum-dyed hair presented a bizarre image. Only eight years old, she carried herself like a sophisticated fashion model.

Gracie's mother had an enormous cleavage, and a blonde, lacquered bouffant hairdo with black roots. Her first question was: "Has Gracie been acting different lately?"

I mentioned the glue bottle incident.

This was her explanation: A while ago, Gracie and her mother returned home from Food City to find her dad in bed "shakin' the sheets" with a woman neighbour. He had been drinking steadily since his release from jail a month earlier, and was finding it extremely tough to find a job.

When Gracie's mom started to scream, he casually walked across the room and split her nose with an ashtray. Gracie ran out of the room. Her mother told me the scar from the incident was carefully hidden under a thick layer of make-up, and she pointed to her nose.

Gracie's dad moved out. He ended up living two floors below, with the other woman. Gracie would periodically bump into him in the elevator. To avoid him, she used the stairs—even though she lived on the twelfth floor.

What chagrined Gracie's mother the most was that all the neighbours told her that her husband was a fool, that she was so much better looking. The other woman "has absolutely nothin up front to make things interestin, if you catch my drift. My husband must be a real blind jerk. I'm the laughin stock of the buildin!

"Can you imagine how I feel? Like a bloody fool. This two-bit floosie comes in and does a number with my man—right under my friggin nose at that! He decides for hamburger when he could be getting a steak! Fine! Let him starve himself to death!"

Gracie had thrown the heavy glue pot at Pasquale because his mother was the woman Gracie's dad had moved in with.

Friday, November 3

Faith was so hungry one day she brought a bottle of Kraft Thousand Island dressing to class and drank over half of it. Then somebody grabbed it away at recess.

Her mother usually wore an expensive blouse or sweater, sporty cord pants and high fashion shoes. Faith usually wore an old over-sized tee-shirt, patched jeans and worn sneakers.

Faith's mother showed up at the school today to ask me if I thought Faith had any acting potential. According to Faith's mother, "There's a lot of big bucks in kids' commercials. It's worth the fifty bucks you have to pay at the beginnin."

Wednesday, November 8

Supply teachers usually claimed to be sick when asked to fill in at our school. And who could blame them? (One supply lasted only fifteen minutes in my classroom.)

As everyone knows, a supply teacher is fair game. And Mr. Cummings was a brand-new supply teacher. He arrived early and eager. He'd never been to our school before, but you could tell he was bursting with enthusiasm.

Later that morning, I heard somebody screaming. I peeked into the classroom where the sound came from, and could hardly believe my eyes. Standing in the centre of the room, dressed in bright green leotards and carrying a crossbow, was Mr. Cummings! A sheepskin vest and Alpine hat completed the outfit.

The costume was part of Mr. Cumming's innovative teaching. He was trying to tell the class the story of William Tell. I suppose he thought the kids would be bowled over by his colourful outfit and style and would spread excited stories of his fantastic lesson! Instead, the kids were laughing and shrieking "Fairy boy!" and "Fag!" and mincing about in front of him. Poor Mr. Cummings.

He slipped his pants on over the leotards while I watched. Then he put a hundred math questions on the board. He didn't say another word.

He advised the office that he would not be available in future.

Monday, November 13

Cecelia, a beautiful West Indian child in my class, has sickle cell anemia. The disease keeps her absent for weeks at a time. Her eyes are yellowy from the daily destruction of her blood cells.

Cecelia bears her pain stoically. When she is pushed, shoved, or knocked over in gym, she never uses her disease as a crutch. Then, after hours, I find her alone at her desk, crying in agony and fear.

Thursday, November 16

A parent stormed into school. He had to let off some steam, because he was fed up with the kids who have been hounding him. The kids live in the townhouse next to his. "Those kids!" he complained. "They live like pigs! They ain't got no respect for the human race!"

He told me that, as a teacher, I should be on guard at all times. He explained that seemingly loyal dogs sometimes turn on their masters for no apparent reason. "And blacks! They contaminate everything they touch! Don't let them breathe in your face!"

If the kids' families "got problems," he didn't want to hear about it. "Let those people booze away their lives with no jobs . . . just because they're too lazy to take the jobs you see advertised. Just look at the want ads! There are plenty of jobs! And besides, the wine they're soppin up each day was paid for by me! That's right—by me!"

He barely stopped to take a breath.

"You should see all the money the government takes off my cheque each week so them winos can buy their bottles of brain rot! Their lives are paid for by the sweat of the work-ingman's brow! Damn foreigners come into this country and take away jobs from real Canadians! Went into their garage next door and let the air outta their tires! That's so he'll learn not to park so close to the sidewalk!

"And I own a gun. Bought it last Saturday when some-body broke the latch on my gate and made off with the barbeque. Don't ever want to have to use it, mind you. But just let one of them jungle bunnies cross over onto my property—then we'll see what happens!"

Friday, November 17

Although I was experiencing considerably more success with the kids, I was beginning to feel uncertain as to how effectively their needs were being met—you could do things, but so much is beyond your control.

Most of the kids in my class faced hardships I'd never had to imagine coping with. Education should give every kid a chance to succeed. And I feared the prejudice and hostility of the society "out there" that would make life rougher for them.

I was lucky; I was white and middle-class; I owned my home in the fashionable "Beaches"; I was well-educated; I held a place in society.

The more I brooded about it, the more anti-social and withdrawn I became. I stopped eating in the lunch room, preferring instead to eat alone in the nearby Italian restaurant. I wondered what else I could do to earn a living beside teach.

This evening I wrote a letter to the university, inquiring about their PhD program in education. I wasn't sure how serious I was about doing more post-grad work, but at least it would provide me with an alternative to the classroom, and I would still be involved with kids.

Monday, November 20
Priscilla brought a picture of her newborn sister, Olivia, to school.

"How d'ya like her?" she asked Samantha.

"Looks like she's gonna turn out white, just like your mom!" Samantha exclaimed.

"But she might grow darker later, like my dad."

"If it turns out white, I'll give you my Barbie doll jumpsuit. If it gets dark by the end of the year, you gimme your Barbie halter top!"

"Deal!"

Tuesday, November 21
Dale had a mother whose wan face came alive when she remembered her life as a little girl on a farm: "Those were the best days of my life."

We were talking after class. Dale was aimlessly kicking a scrap of paper the caretaker had missed on his four o'clock round. I had asked his mother to come in because I wanted to know more about Dale's home life.

"I wish we were still living on a farm," she continued. "That's what I regret most—not raising Dale in the country." Suddenly she was brushing away tears from her cheeks.

Dale looked embarrassed and left the room. "I want something out of life for Dale, but I just don't know how I can do it. He's still upset about his father leaving, and he just won't seem to settle down. I'm out working and I don't really have time for him when I get home. You don't know what factory work is like. It sucks all the energy out of you, so I don't have that much left over for him."

Dale reappeared and sat in a chair near the window. His mother started talking again, but soon broke down.

"Look," I said, doing my best to reassure her any way I could, "I'll do my best to keep Dale out of trouble in school. Try not to worry."

When they left, Dale shot me a quick smile. Somebody's fist had punched out one of his teeth. It was his first smile of the term.

Wednesday, November 22

Mickey wasn't doing his assignment; he complained his arm was sore. When I asked him what was wrong with it, he replied, "It has bad germs in it."

"Okay, Mickey," I said. "Roll up your sleeve so I can see where the 'bad germs' are."

He could barely pull his sleeve past his elbow. With my help, we inched the sleeve up higher, revealing a pussy sore. It looked like a face.

Mickey explained: "I asked T.J. to give me a tattoo like all the other kids. I wanted a 'screamin skull.'" His brother had carved a skull into Mickey's arm, using a pin and some ink "he leaked out of a pen."

Mickey was too embarrassed to go to the school nurse. I had to insist.

Monday, December 4

A friend of mine introduced me to a teacher from British Columbia who was in Toronto for a speaking engagement.

She worked with disadvantaged kids herself, and was starting up a new magazine to deal with "teaching and capitalism." Before she left, we made arrangements to meet over a drink. She was a stunningly beautiful woman of about thirty, with something very compelling about the way she spoke.

At a nearby "working-class" tavern she told me over a beer that most curriculum materials presently used in classrooms cue and condition working-class readers to behave in certain ways: to have negative self-images, to believe in the inevitability of their lot in life, to perceive their predicament in an isolated way, and to regard the possibility of change in the class structure as futile, or at least merely wishful thinking. She maintained that as my kids grew up, they would become more and more aware of how much their social class places them outside of the "mainstream of society."

Over another round of beer she talked about class differences. "Your kids are too young for you to make them socially active. But already you can see what's happening to them as a result of their poverty. It must upset you, as a teacher, to feel so damned helpless! They sit in front of the TV and soak in all the advertisements for expensive clothes, toys, delicious food . . . while they go back home for a Kraft Dinner lunch and a coke!"

Protesting that things weren't that hopeless, I outlined some of the units I was using in class to promote self-concept, understanding and harmony. But I had to admit they weren't working very effectively.

"You're still working within the capitalist ideology!" she remarked, grabbing my arm in a friendly gesture, almost knocking over her draft in the process. "You're romanticizing the idea that people share a fundamental humanity that occurs through a common understanding. But, under the capitalist system, this basic humanity is perverted because the class structure of our society denies working-class kids equal opportunities. You're merely accommodating inequality."

I had to remind her several times that I was teaching seven- and eight-year-olds, and that nothing I could do in one year, even if I agreed with her philosophy, would dramatically change their lives.

"Kids who grow up feeling hopeless," she said, her voice rising, "become self-effacing and self-deprecating. If you can't reach your class because they're too young, then get your parents together! Organize them!"

Although I oppose Marxism as such, I couldn't help wondering if there wasn't a lot of truth in what she was saying.

Monday, December 11

I didn't notice Mickey leave. I sent some of the kids to find out where he had vanished to. They had one hell of a time finding him.

Finally, they noticed a pair of tiny brown shoes under the cubicle doors in the boy's washroom. When they opened the door, they found Mickey asleep on the toilet.

Wednesday, December 13

Charlotte's group of ten perceptually handicapped kids wanted to repay me for taking them on a field trip to the waterfront. She suggested to them that a fun way to say "thanks" would be to make me up a nice hot lunch.

Mad Sid became the most excited. Mad Sid earned his name by jumping out of a second storey window—and surviving without a scratch. Charlotte always had to keep one eye on him.

She took her kids down to the staff room kitchen. The idea was to surprise me with a spaghetti lunch, the recipe contributed by Mad Sid's mother.

Chester the Hypo(chondriac) was especially eager to

help make the sauce. Like Mad Sid, he could be difficult in class. He complained daily that he had everything from an upset stomach to a brain tumour. He complained to Charlotte that Sid's mother probably put something poisonous in the recipe, warning her to watch out for suspicious-looking stuff.

There was a critical element in the recipe they didn't know about: I had a meeting with a parent during my lunch hour. I was, in fact, particularly eager to get that interview over with. Brad's mother always spieled out her woes for what felt like hours.

When I arrived, she was sitting on the staff room sofa looking as theatrical as ever. In her mid-forties, she was a platinum blonde (this time) and her eyebrows were plucked into thin half-circles.

"Sit over here, please, Mr. McLaren," she began at once. "I've a lot to talk about. Now, about Brad—"

Charlotte's kids had sneaked into the kitchen while I began my conversation with Brad's mother. On a signal from Charlotte, they formed a line, and with Sid in the lead holding the pot of steaming spaghetti, they marched into the staff room.

"All right!" Mad Sid ordered. "Right face!"

Everyone swung around.

"Ready, troops? Let's go!"

As they marched up between us, they made quite a sight. Mad Sid was wearing army fatigues and a plastic German army helmet. Chester wore a pink 1950s sports jacket that came down to his knees and a pair of Charlotte's black leotards, which he claimed were giving him a rash. A kid named Sweeney was carrying the cutlery in a straw basket suspended from his mouth. He peered out at everybody through a pair of moss-green diving goggles. Candy, who was carrying up the rear, sported a black velvet opera cape and shook a noisy tambourine. I pretended to be embarrassed by this weird procession, but Charlotte knew I loved every minute of it!

Brad's mother watched in growing consternation the classic cast of kids. She rose to her feet, dramatically threw her coat around her shoulders, and paused at the door to tell me, "I'll be in touch with you when you ain't playing no zoo keeper!"

It was a great lunch.

Monday, December 18

A few weeks ago, I decided to try a new strategy for stopping fights. Whenever two kids started to throw punches, I gathered the entire class around the combatants, and we all hummed the old "look sharp" Gillette Friday Night Fight theme. It was so silly, the fighters started to laugh. I broke up a lot of fights in class that way.

Rod told me that he was going to submit the idea to HAID (Humane Alternatives in Discipline), an organization of teachers and parents who opposed corporal punishment.

Wednesday, December 20

Yesterday, when Fred saw me wearing overalls stained with paint from the previous evening's art therapy course, and carrying some of the latest school journals under my arm, he laughed. "If you don't slow down and lay off a bit, you're going to steal my act!"

Some of the staff members, however, were raising more than merely curious eyebrows at my apparent headlong plunge into putting Fred's philosophy into action so overtly. As long as the "strange goings-on" were confined to my classroom, they didn't object, but when I let the kids work in the hall or staff room, they felt threatened. The few teachers on staff who didn't really approve of Fred's approach felt he was filling the staff with "hippies"—me, for example—and at the staff meeting, with both Fred and Rod absent, they decided it was the opportune moment to nail me. They took me totally by surprise.

"I hear music coming from your class a lot, Peter. What kind of courses are you teaching?" one of them asked.

"Young kids need to be controlled. I'm going to get some of your hellions next year, and I don't want them running wild all over *my* class," another contributed.

"And why are you letting your kids work out in the halls?" one teacher demanded in a peremptory tone, rising out of her chair.

I was startled, and didn't know how to react to all this hostility.

John tried to come to my rescue. "Are they disturbing your kids?" he asked one of the irate teachers.

"Well ... not exactly ... but some of us have seen Peter's kids making his breakfast in the staff room! And they were unsupervised."

I found myself rising slowly out of my chair. "There were some grade six kids supervising the cooking," I said, trying to remain calm. "They weren't making my breakfast; they happened to be making their own breakfasts, because they didn't get a breakfast that morning or a dinner the previous night!" My voice was rising, but I couldn't hold back. "And if you're worried about the school budget, you can rest easy. The money for the eggs and oatmeal came out of my pocket!"

I called Fred later to tell him I'd had it.

"Peter, I want you at the school for as long as I'm there. And if you alter your program one iota, I'll fire you!" he reassured me.

Charlotte and Liz, buddies of mine, admitted they were too shocked at the staff meeting to say anything. To give me a lift, they treated me to a spaghetti lunch at the best Italian restaurant in the Corridor, and presented me with a gift. "It's to help you get over yesterday's staff meeting," Charlotte said.

It was a book on biofeedback, and how to generate peaceful mind waves.

Friday, December 22

I enjoyed celebrating Christmas with the kids. The class spent hours decorating the room with Christmas posters I was given or had bought. A plastic tree was donated by a previous staff member, and we decorated it with crepe paper, tinsel, popcorn and cotton batting.

I played some Christmas carols on my guitar, not very well, I'm afraid, since I usually play only the blues. But we all sang together, and it felt very Christmassy.

The kids had shown up with presents for me: socks, wallets, bottles of wine, chocolates, beer mugs, well over half the class brought something for me. I had stressed that presents didn't matter, but I could see Mickey was upset because he didn't have anything for me. When he saw all the other kids giving me gifts, he ran out of the room.

About fifteen minutes later, he returned with a plastic bag. "This is a Christmas present for you," he said, handing me the bag, head lowered.

"Thanks, Mickey," I replied, cordially. He walked over to his desk and stood there, sort of squirming. "Why don't you come over here while I open it?" I suggested.

He took a few steps, then stopped.

I reached into the bag and pulled out a tattered copy of *National Geographic.* I immediately recognized it as one of the many I kept in the stockroom.

"Thanks, Mickey!" I exclaimed. "Just what I need for my collection."

"I . . . I," he stuttered. "I bought it at the store yesterday. Cost me five bucks."

"How did you know it was my favourite magazine?"

"Cause it's got naked black people inside."

The class laughed, and we all went on with the Christmas festivities.

Samantha, slouched despondently in her chair, refused to join in. All the kids were eating pizza and playing their favourite disco tunes on the record player, but she ignored them. Every so often she would look at someone with a sideways glance, but mostly she stared glumly ahead.

"What's wrong, Samantha?" I asked, coming over when I had the chance. "Why aren't you joining the party?"

She looked up at me, her eyes dark and surly. "My head's playin funny tricks again."

"Tricks?"

"It's that person in my head." Her voice was choked with anger. "Somebody's inside and won't leave!" She whirled around in her seat, contemptuously swept her hand through her dreadlocks and rose out of the chair. Then she began trembling. "The voice keeps telling me about the end of the world, so there won't be no more Christmas, or summer, or winter or nothin!" Normally, she was not this disturbed.

"Look, Samantha, why on earth are you thinking of such awful things? This is Christmas time! It's happy!"

"My dad told me the world was gonna end soon, and Jesus was gonna come back." She fidgeted nervously.

"Try to think of something nice," I tried reassuringly. "I'm sure if Jesus did come back, he'd be an okay guy. You wouldn't get hurt."

"On Saturday, this voice told me to gets rid of my sister friend, so I don't play with her no more. I likes my best friend, but this voice inside me told me she's bad." Her tone was so bitter.

"Who do you think the voice is?"

Her eyes dilated slightly. "It's the devil."

"Why do you think that?"

"My dad says the devil is strong and can go inside people's heads, and makes them think bad thoughts." Then she started to cry.

I put my arms around her. "Are you sure it's the devil and not just your imagination?" I was at a loss as to how to handle this.

"I . . . I don't know." She wiped away the tears. "I think so. Can you makes the voices go way?"

"Well, I don't know, but I'll have a talk with your dad this evening. Anyway," I continued, "I'm sure that God is stronger than the devil. So don't you worry so much."

I gave her a gentle push, and after a moment got her dancing. Half and hour later, she was the most enthusiastic dancer on the floor.

I called her dad tonight and told him the story. At my suggestion, he agreed to play down the devil and accent the more positive aspects of his beliefs.

Friday, December 29

An old friend of mine named Phil, who teaches in an inner-city school in Winnipeg, visited Jenny and me during the Christmas holidays. I brought out a bottle of Phil's favourite gin, and we talked late into the evening. Phil, as usual, was not at a loss for words, and he wasted no time in leading the discussion.

"So many kids in this country are emotionally starved," he told me. "Most of the kids I see pass through my door seem so wholly defeated and demoralized by life. They're filled with fear, suspicion, anger, hatred, you name it. The wounds of their souls are rubbed raw and torn open each day. Schools have to make these kids feel that they're human beings and worth something.

"I end up doing what you're doing, Peter; I end up functioning both as teacher and therapist. As a teacher, I try to inculcate a love of learning and impart knowledge and skills, and unfold some creative capacities. But as a thera-pist, I have to reduce so much excessive anxiety in these kids and try to dissolve so many emotional blocks that I'm becoming an emotional wreck myself!"

"Aren't we, as teachers, partially responsible for caus-ing some of the problems?" I asked. "I mean . . . we support a system of education that's obviously failing the kids. What can we do when we're given thirty-five kids to teach in a crowded classroom who have already developed a mistrust and hatred for the world?"

Phil was always ready with an answer. "We've got to get the support of the community; we have to make them realize that their kids aren't getting a fair shake. And listen, that includes all kids; they've got just as many problems as your immigrant kids. People are too ready to believe the poor are all welfare cheaters, or lazy, or that they keep having illegitimate children to get more mother's allowance cheques. Somehow we've got to bridge that gap between the world of ghetto kids and the middle-class pablum game of school."

We talked about the growing violence in the schools.

He shrugged his shoulders and breathed deeply. "Like jails and looney bins, schools isolate students from the real problems going on out there in society. I often wonder whether schools aren't just simply glorified baby-sitting institutions. . . . Look at it this way. We don't really need more manpower, and schools just delay the time the kids have to get out there and find jobs.

"Students are frustrated and feel like they don't belong. We expose them to aggressive models of success and then scream 'achieve! achieve!' until they turn off. And when they fail in school, they feel like failures in life. Look at what they're exposed to: TV, radio, newspapers, magazines, movies, ads, I could go on and on. Then we drop these over-stimulated kids into the slowest-moving institution in our society—our schools.

"Anyway, I'm beginning to sound like a textbook, as usual. Time for another drink. Am I pouring or are you?"

Monday, January 8
Dean, the school librarian, quit his job. He told me he simply couldn't take the kids any more—the noise level was unbearable. His new job is out in Moose Jaw, Saskatchewan, teaching at a private school.

A number of staff applied for Dean's job, and by secret ballot Helen, a special education teacher, was elected. I owe much of my sanity to her reorganization of the library.

Helen realized that, for inner-city kids, libraries were often boring places, and a library had to be a place for more than simply reading books. She set about changing the library from a place to *read* into a place to *do*.

Working late into the evenings, she set up over twenty activity areas where kids could work with sand, water or blocks. They could also make their own newspapers, play with hockey cards, research just about any topic, make comics, tape stories, act out their own dramas on a make-shift stage, even play with the variety of puppets Helen had created. She arranged a schedule enabling a teacher to send a maximum of ten kids at a time each day. The kids loved the library more than anything else, with the possible exception of Big Arnie's room.

It was such a relief to be minus ten kids for half an hour! But more important, the kids learned a lot there (whether they realized it or not); it was obvious from their projects and completed assignments. I was thankful for Helen; she had made a real difference.

Friday, January 12

Suzanne was dropped off at my door late this morning by her father. He wore a green snowmobile suit and a black cap with "Davey Boy" stitched in yellow across the brim, and he reeked of booze. "Suzanne hurt her leg this morning. Here," he grumbled, thrusting her toward me.

She hobbled up to my desk, eyes sunken into reddened sockets. Her father muttered goodbye through a half-smile of blackened teeth.

"That cocksucker!" Suzanne cried when he was gone. "He cracked me right across my leg with a stick just cause I wouldn't let him take my babysittin money! Now he'll just go and buy another bottle!"

Tuesday, January 16

Mickey spent half the art period modelling his clay into a hot dog. When he finished, he walked to the front of the class and proudly showed it to me. Then he pretended to eat it, smacking his lips.

"That's too big for a hot dog!" Marta complained.

"My mom's got a plastic thing at home that looks like Mickey's hot dog," Chastity chimed in. "Only hers got bumps on it, and a battery inside to make it shake!"

Tuesday, January 23

Some parents were hard to draw to the school for interviews. If their kids weren't behaviour problems, the parents usually showed up on interview night. But the parents I really wanted to see—whose kids were absolutely uncontrollable—rarely appeared (even if they had signed the interview consent form).

This evening, as I sat alone perking coffee on a rented machine, a woman wandered into my room. She identified herself as Mrs. Bailey; she was drunk.

"You Mr. Hartford?"

"No, I'm sorry."

"Oh well, then." She didn't seem to mind. As a matter of fact, it seemed to make no difference at all. She began to talk, slowly at first, picking up velocity as she went along. "You see, when I get home after workin late . . . it's like . . . the reason I get so pissed off is on account of . . . the reason I get so mad is because. . . .

"I get home from work and nobody's there to say hello—except the kids. Oh ya, and two friggin goldfish that Bobby never changes the water for. Big deal. Two goldfish and two kids.

"First thing I do when I get home is check if Bobby's changed the water in the tank. Christ, the tank cost me more than the fish! Sometimes when the tank's dirty, I feel like flushin those two goddam fish down the toilet. God knows they'd be better off.

"Who wants to work their ass off all day an not know what's gonna happen that night?—you tell me that! Got an answer for that one? Who's gonna take out a separated mother with two kids? Especially Wendy, the three-year-old. I mean, Bobby's okay. He takes care of Wendy when I'm at work . . . gets his free room an board, don't he?

"Nobody in my damn buildin wants to babysit for under a buck an hour, and if you say you'll return the favour, you get cornered for the whole fuckin evening. They don't come back until sun-up, an they ain't even got the bloody decency to phone!

"I mean . . . put it this way. . . ." She smoothed her coat collar, then plunged back in. "I've babysat for some of those bitches who don't give a shit if they never see their little brats again. You got the picture? So alls my time's spent at home . . . never one bloody night off. Can you believe it? This ole lady is getting tired . . . getting tired. . . .

"Eight o'clock rolls around an I'm back at it. I work the double shift sometimes, so I don't get home till after ten, see. An what's goin on? Bobby's taken off and he forgets all about Wendy. If anythin happens to Wendy I told him I'd have his balls in a basket.

"When I'm there at the plant after the double shift, sometimes Rick gives me a drive home early, he's a friend of mine. Asks himself up for a drink and makes out like him and Bobby are good buddies—father and son—just so he can get into my pants. Men sure are hard up these days for manners. No way I'm gonna fall for that one. I told him already that men still have to prove themselves. That means hands off, baby! Hands off the merchandise!

"When was the last time I got out to the Swiss Chalet? Sure wasn't with Rick, lemme tell you! Cheap bastard. One time, only one time he takes me over to Fran's on College. And you know what that's full of these days. Fags! Yah, you heard me! Queers!

"Last time he tried to put the make on me was in his car. His car! Can you believe it? So here I am, after the double shift, and the kids keep complainin that there's nothin to eat and I tell them they must be blind cause there's all these boxes of Kraft Dinner. . . .

"Kids today are so goddamn lazy. Makes me want to scream. . . ."

Wednesday, January 31

Well, all right. I do have a tendency to rattle on during a lesson. But this time, I had barely started when I noticed that Samantha looked bored. She was sitting at her desk, in deep thought. Her head moved from side to side as if she were struggling against an insistent voice inside her. I could see the muscles along her jaws tense as she seemed to forcibly stop herself from speaking.

As I went on with the lesson, I kept an eye on her.

She looked down, nervously tapping on her desk. Then her hands suddenly jerked back and she shot to her feet, with both eyes bulging. When she had everyone's startled attention, she began to sing in a rather sweet voice:

"As I was walkin down the lane, shh shh
I met a pretty girl in Spain, shh shh
When she leaned against the wall, shh shh
I gives her my balls and all, shh shh
Wouldn't momma be surprised, shh shh
To see her belly-button rise, shh shh
Won't momma be sad, shh shh
When she finds dad's mad, shh shh
Mommy on the bottom
Daddy on the top
Baby in the middle
Saying give it all you got!"

Suddenly the room was filled with dancing kids. So much for my lesson!

Tuesday, February 6

Angie's mother, looking very worried, came in this afternoon and told me that a child had been molested in the elevator of her apartment building. (Half my class lived in that building.) From tomorrow on, she would pick up Angie and her sisters from school every afternoon, and escort them home to make sure nothing happened to them. "I'm going to do this every day, every week, every month of the year, for as long as my kids go to school," she told me, her voice filled with worry and anger. "If Angie has any work to finish after school, you'll just have to send it home with her."

She expected Angie to meet her in the school lobby at three-fifteen every afternoon. She wanted to have all her children safe inside their apartment by three-thirty. The molestation had taken place at four o'clock.

Friday, February 9

Tasha, a grade six student from Mrs. Rogers' class, enjoyed staying after school to help me clean up my room. Mrs. Rogers was delighted that Tasha had taken a liking to me—she needed a male figure at this point in her life. Her father had recently walked out.

Always pale, with red, sad-looking eyes, Tasha shuffled listlessly around my room each afternoon, picking up scrap paper and depositing it in the wastepaper basket. Every day she wore the same powder-blue denim dress, worn thin at the elbows.

Somewhere Tasha acquired a whisk broom, which she briskly used on the carpet. Down on her knees to brush chalk, she was very much the figure of Cinderella before the fairy-godmother arrived. After gathering all the debris into the wastepaper basket, she would carry it awkwardly down the stairs and empty it in the caretaker's office.

As soon as she finished, she would make a beeline for the art centre I had set up at the back of the room. She always chose to play with modelling clay, shaping it into a figure resembling a man wearing a hat, carrying a suitcase. When I asked her who the figure was, she said only that it was "a traitor." After completing the figure, she would then viciously tear it apart.

She seemed to get a strange kind of comfort from the time she spent with me, but after a few weeks, Tasha no longer showed up to help with my room. Some of the other kids, I heard, had been teasing her about having a crush on me.

Monday, February 12

I met Priscilla's mother in the shopping mall at lunchtime. "Are you Mr. McLaren?" she said, her eyes wide and sparkling. "I'm Priscilla's mother."

"How are you?"

"I'm feelin a lot better these days. The ladies in my buildin finally got together this week and we had a meetin in the basement." Her eyes roved over my face, a steaming hot dog clenched in her fist. "Well . . . a lot of us are gettin fed up with nothin happenin around here. We decided to take things into our own hands, so we're trying to set up some kind of day care for our kids. I mean, we got to do *somethin!*" She paused to watch a group of teenagers with large blaring transistors wander by, looking at clothing displays in the store windows, punctuating the raucous music with a burst of "cool threads!" "Look at those leathers!"

"That sounds great. Do you think you'll be able to do it?" I asked.

"We can if we really try—we've had it if we don't. I mean, who's goin to look after the baby when I'm at work? Priscilla's at school and nobody else is around. Anyway, I was glad to see everybody really tryin to help each other instead of the usual bitchin."

I wished her good luck and she shook my hand.

"Good luck to you, too," she said. "You know, you got half the kids from my buildin in your class!"

Tuesday, February 20

A conversation I had with Marta's mother about her first night in the city, in the Jane-Finch area, sticks in my mind:

"We had just moved into the city from Tillsonburg," she began. "You know, a farming-type community. Well, it was our first real overnight in the new townhouse, and all of us were tickled to death, if you know what I mean.

"The furniture didn't arrive and we had to sleep right on the floor, but I told the kids to pretend it was just like camping in a brick tent.

"In the morning my husband, George, heard this knock on the door. When he opened it, he saw this bottle on the porch with a piece of burning rag crackling and sticking out of the top . . . one of those molotov cocktails you see in the war movies? Well! George just gives it a big kick, and the bottle goes flying onto the sidewalk. The rag pops out and lands away from all that spilled gasoline, so nothing burned. Later, I found out that the next-door neighbour put it there."

"Did you talk to your neighbour about it?"

"Oh yes, we're good friends now. You see, the bomb was really for the former tenants. They had this child that kept the neighbour up all night. It had colic or something. It was our neighbour's way of saying, shut that kid up! You see, he didn't realize those people and their kids had already moved out, and we'd moved in."

Monday, February 26

I had been getting depressed again. From the moment I woke up, I dreaded the thought of going to school. I found myself puttering around the house each morning: doing dishes, reading a book, finding any excuse not to leave until the very last minute. Usually I arrived at the school only moments before the bell.

Fred began to mention that I was "cutting my arrivals pretty close," so I decided to make a concerted effort to arrive early. Perhaps I could work out some material before the kids arrived: I could prepare the room, have the work already on the blackboard, flesh out my lesson plan. Maybe more advance preparation would get me in a better frame of mind.

So I set my alarm for six-thirty, and if I rushed breakfast and traffic wasn't a problem, I could make it to the school before eight.

Every morning a miserable-looking kid, a little black boy wearing a rumpled brown jacket and a Super Fly cap, was always standing in the same spot in the teachers' parking lot. Sometimes he whistled loudly, sometimes he hummed.

After the first few days, I decided he was trying to attract my attention. Usually I just gave him a wave or a smile. Now I began to invite him to come inside with me. He timidly introduced himself as Ralph, but I nicknamed him "Early Bird"—Bird for short.

He showed his appreciation by eagerly dashing around my room, tidying my cupboards, scrubbing graffiti off desk tops, placing a freshly run-off mimeo sheet at each desk. After about half an hour of helping out, he'd curl up on my desk like a mongrel pup, tired and hungry.

He apologized for tiring out so fast. "It's because I never get to sleep till late—an I don't have no breakfast. Everythin's crazy in the mornin at my house. But I gotta lunch," he said, brightening up. I looked in the bag: nothing more than a few stale cookies. To combat hunger pangs he always carries a small brown envelope filled with jello powder, taking huge mouthfulls when he needs a lift.

I promised to give Bird some fresh fruit every day if he gave up on the jello powder, and we struck a bargain. He would become my permanent morning helper in exchange for the fresh fruit I brought him.

Thursday, March 1

I was startled when Rod commented on the way I was dressing for work: bottle-green railroad overalls, Birkenstock sandals, lumberjack shirt. "You look just like the kids!" he explained, trying an engaging smile. "Maybe that's why they like you so much; they can't tell you apart from their classmates. When you first started teaching here, you were as straight as an arrow. Now you look more like a hippie!"

I was glad that the administration had a flexible dress code for the staff. I first began switching my dress pants and sports jackets to casual clothes for practical reasons: my good clothes always got covered in paint or torn when I tried to break up fights. One of my favourite jackets had to be thrown out when I found magic marker swipes all over the back.

Now I wear casual clothes more for comfort. I also figured I could relate to the kids better if I didn't distance myself from them by wearing expensive clothes. I knew I was on the right track when a kid remarked, nodding at my attire: "You really look neat, sir! You dress just like my dad does when he goes on shift at the factory!"

At least half the staff are now wearing jeans. Several teachers who are very fashion conscious objected to the "deterioration" in teacher image. They made a formal protest to Fred and Rod, requesting that teachers be forbidden to wear jeans, except for field trips or extra-curricular sports. When the administration refused to make any such rule, the protesting teachers grew even more upset. They're muttering about transferring to other schools, not wishing to be associated with a school full of "beatniks."

Tuesday, March 6

My gas tank was bone dry when I tried to start my van this afternoon. Sighing, empty container in hand, I headed off towards the nearest gas station.

My route took me through the housing project that some of my kids called "the zoo." Kids were all over the sidewalks and yards. I saw a few of them climbing a TV antenna that ran up the side of a townhouse. Another group of young children piled into a stolen shopping cart that was then pushed into the street. Passing cars swerved to a shrieking halt, narrowly missing the kids. "Ya fuckin kids! Get off the fuckin streets!" a driver yelled at them.

I passed a group of teenagers slumped on the sidewalk, waving a can of something in the air. On my way back I passed the same group and one of them shouted: "Hey mister! You gonna get high on all that gas?" I grinned and kept walking.

A kid of about ten grabbed a screaming toddler by the hair and dragged him into a nearby townhouse as I walked by. "Get in the goddam house before I fry your balls off on the stove!" The door slammed.

Friday, March 16

The primary division teachers spend a lot of time together as a group. Some of the other teachers feel the primary staff are too much of a clique, but as far as I can see, the group stays together for mutual support in planning for the kids, not to form an elite of any kind.

One of the primary teachers, Liz, is an expert in child psychology. She is also gorgeous, an absolutely stunning woman with long, jet black hair cascading down to her slender waist. During my first two years, she barely acknowledged that I was alive, except for the usual daily pleasantries about the weather. Now that I'm a primary teacher, she spends less time with the other primary teachers and more and more time with me.

We worked out a program for the kids in which we switch classes several times a week. She takes my kids for a traditional music period, and I take hers for a game of murderball in the gym.

Liz provides the kids with an opportunity to let their fantasies about teachers run wild. Each time she comes into the room, some of my kids shout out: "Sir loves Liz! He told us just a minute ago!" and "I'm tellin the principal you guys neck in class!"

I tried to explain that Liz and I were both happily married—to other people.

"That don't matter," Mickey yelled. "Lots of folks in my buildin are married, but they still fool aroun!"

"Yah!" Frank agreed. "Just don't tell your wife!"

One day, one of her kids knocked on my door and handed me a note, explaining that someone had given her the note to give to Liz. When I opened it I saw a carefully drawn picture of an erect penis. Written below: "Liz, I want to love you tonight." It was signed with my name.

Teachers have to watch their every step.

Wednesday, March 28

At John's suggestion, I'd begun instruction in Tai Chi, a Chinese form of exercise somewhat resembling Kung Fu, except that all the movements are performed in slow motion and it's used only for defence. Since the exercises are noted for having a calming effect (they certainly helped me), I decided to teach some Tai Chi after class to Mickey, who found it difficult to keep still in class, even for five minutes at a time.

After the first few sessions, Mickey quickly grew bored and restless. I mentioned this to Fred, who offered to work with Mickey after school. He felt confident he would discover some new technique which would help Mickey.

Fred approached me this morning with a grin on his face. "Mickey and I have been working together for almost an hour every day after school this week," he proudly said. "He sits quietly and concentrates throughout the entire session."

"Wow! What are you doing? Tai Chi? Yoga? Zen?"

He smiled. "It's called playing checkers."

Monday, April 2

Ros handed me a shiny, cracked snapshot of her home town in Nicaragua. Her grandmother was standing outside of a cinderblock house, smiling at the camera.

Standing next to the house was a church that looked as if it was made from corrugated aluminum. Pointing to the church, Ros exclaimed: "God rests there on his trips round the world!"

Next to the church stood her father, wearing a moss-green military uniform and holding a sub-machine gun. "He shoots the people who robs the stores."

Standing next to him was a hollow-cheeked woman. "That's my mother. My sister just died—she was only three an she made my mother cry and cry."

I looked at the photo for a long time.

"All the kids tease me cause I talk funny," Ros finally said. "I wanna go back home."

Thursday, April 12

Teachers can order special marking stamps from a supply catalogue or retailer. Usually the stamps bear standard captions: "Excellent," "Good work," "Do over," "Neater please," and so forth. A little cartoon figure usually accompanies each caption. Priscilla stole one of my stamps that had an angel on it. The angel was holding up a scroll which read "You can do better."

She was found with my angel stamp in the girl's washroom, stamping sheet after sheet of toilet paper.

Tuesday, April 17

This morning there was a violent wind storm. Kids on their way to school were literally blown across the streets, cars had to pull over to the curb and garbage littered the sidewalks. Naturally, few kids showed up for school, only ten in my class. Most of them wanted a free day in the library to work on projects of their own choice, so I gave them my permission. Only Colin wanted to stay in the classroom.

Characteristically quiet and sullen, he was now unusually talkative. He began to tell me stories of what he was doing, how on weekends he took a plane to either the White House or Elvis Presley's gravesite . . . depending on how he felt. He spoke very seriously.

With the wind howling outside, he began to talk about his sleepwalking. He said his mother would find him out in the hall in the middle of the night, pounding his fists against the wall. Then he told me about how he almost murdered a little girl.

"I get this funny feelin inside of me," he said slowly. "It's like somebody else comes inside my body. When I get this feelin, I feel like I want to kill somebody. One night I saw this little girl down by the creek, and I almost killed her with my pen knife. I would've killed her, too, if her brother hadn't come along. My mom and dad went to court with me, afterwards."

I didn't know what to think.

"Sometimes I dream of blood," Colin continued. "I love blood and guts and things like that. I dream sometimes about kissin blood. That's why I like fightin—all that blood! Once my dad cut his finger with a carving knife at dinner. He din't want blood to drip all over the carpet, so I sucked his finger for him." The wind rattled the windows.

The next day I gave Colin's mother a call. She agreed to contact a clinic for emotionally disturbed kids.

Thursday, April 19

Yesterday, I met with a group of about twenty teachers and principals from fourteen different schools in the city. We were trying to form a committee to investigate ways to help schools further meet the needs of working-class and immigrant children from poor families. Over hot pizza in a public school about a mile outside of the Corridor, we talked about some of our worries and concerns.

Mostly we talked about the mountain of problems immigrant kids have to cope with when adjusting to Canadian schools and way of life: language or dialect barriers; conflicting traditions and customs; culture shock; parental expectations and personal goals; heavy workloads both in school and at home; academic upgrading; family conflicts. These kids were often called names, misunderstood, made to feel inferior.

A grade five teacher told us that recently she was phoned late at night by a parent of one of her students. The parent was a single mother. Alone in her townhouse with her daughter at the time, she became panic-stricken as two adolescent boys tried to break down her door with a crowbar to get at her daughter. The parent demanded that the teacher "do something about it."

Another teacher spoke of two children in her class that were locked outside by their parents in the middle of winter, as punishment.

One teacher told the group in a husky voice, trembling with emotion, that she couldn't bear to see one child bring a lunch, day after day, consisting of only pieces of dried toast.

Each teacher reported a long litany of child abuse and hunger. As the afternoon progressed, we had all shared scores of classroom horror stories.

Up until now, I thought that many of the severe problems that kids had were isolated to my particular class or school district. But after hearing of similar experiences from so many teachers, I knew I wasn't alone.

"There are lots more of us," one teacher told me, "who are afraid to speak out against the conditions in our schools because we're afraid of getting our knuckles rapped for rocking the boat."

Friday, April 20

Like so many other teachers, I joked about quitting after a hard day with the kids. Only now I was beginning to take the idea more seriously. I had been accepted as a doctorate candidate in education, and two years of full-time study was compulsory. That would also mean two full years without earning a regular salary. But it would give me the chance to do some research on inner-city kids, and perhaps work to make changes outside the system.

I reluctantly discussed the idea again with Jenny; my middle-class ideas about being supported by my wife made me uneasy. Perhaps, though, I could get a grant or scholarship.

Jenny listened to me for an hour as I rambled on, trying to put my thoughts in order, awash with despondency and frustration.

She seemed to be on the edge of disapproval when she flung back her hair, a half-smile on her lips. "Hold it. Hold it right there, honey. I've heard all this before, and it's okay. Look, we both agreed that you'd leave when you couldn't hack it anymore, when you couldn't give 100 per cent to the kids. I don't want you to end up like those middle-aged teachers who go through their lessons like robots, all their enthusiasm gone. I mean, that kind of attitude won't help the kids either. Take your doctorate if you want. It's your decision. We'll be able to manage. Hey! There's a good film on TV tomorrow night."

"What?"

"The Blackboard Jungle!"

A sense of humour helps.

Wednesday, April 25

T.J. knocked on my door to give me a warning. "Sir!" he explained. "There's a fire engine parked out the front! A fire drill!" Unannounced fire drills occurred sporadically. Fire marshalls and a truck would always show up just before a drill, so we could always prepare for them.

I turned to the kids and quickly reviewed fire-drill

procedures: no talking, no shoving, no sliding down ban-
nisters. Also, the last person to leave shuts the door.

And then the fire bell began to ring. I swung open the
door and came face-to-face with one of the four fire marshalls supervising the drill. To my embarrassment, Mickey
suddenly broke out of line and shouted: "Lance called me a
cocksucker! I'm gonna give him a punch!"

The fire marshall looked more embarrassed than I was.

"We'll settle it later, Mickey!" I yelled, urging the kids
out the door and down the stairs.

"But sir!" Mickey insisted. He wasn't about to give up,
especially in front of a fire marshall. "He called me a cocksucker!"

By now most of the kids had made their way downstairs
on their own. A few hung around to watch the scene, as
Mickey suddenly grabbed Lance and pounded his head on
the floor screaming, "Goddam welfare prick!" I grabbed
them both, one under each arm, and carried them down the
stairs and out into the yard. The rest of the kids followed.

Once outside, Mickey kicked the wall angrily. "We
didn't have to come outside. You tricked us! Look . . . there's
no fire!"

The fire marshall gave me a rueful glance, tipped his hat
to me, and murmured, "Nice place you got here," and
walked quickly to his car.

Thursday, April 26

A senior administrator on the Board paid a visit to my
classroom. Every few years he makes his rounds, visiting all
the elementary schools in his jurisdiction to pay his respects.
He walked into my room smiling. "Glad to see you!" he said
heartily. "Fine group of kids you got here!" I smiled and
shook hands.

"Like your set-up here," he continued. "Room sure is
colourful." He was short and on the plump side, and he
fingered a cuff-link nervously. "Nice bunch of kids!"

The kids laughed and applauded themselves. "Who's the turkey?" one of them stage-whispered.

Mr. Brooks cleared his throat. "Hear you're doing a good job," he said. I nodded, and he smiled and walked out.

Mickey watched him go, then pulled urgently at my sleeve. "I've seen guys like that before at my house. They come all the time to see my brothers. He's your parole officer, ain't he!"

Friday, April 27

Georgette and Wendy picked up some dolls at the activity centre. Georgette chose a G.I. Joe, and Wendy picked up a Farrah Fawcett doll.

"Let's pretend we're married," Georgette said.

"Okay," Wendy agreed, "let's start!"

Georgette took G.I. Joe's arm and promptly slapped the Farrah doll across the face with it, shouting: "That's what you get for talkin to me like that!"

Monday, April 30

On the weekend I went to a neighbourhood party held in a posh house near the lakefront. I'm not much of a party-goer, but I was feeling weary and depressed, and needed to cut loose a bit.

After downing a stiff martini, I heard a voice behind me say, "I hear you're a teacher."

When I turned, I saw a woman in champagne-coloured kidskin pants and a see-through blouse. "You *are* a teacher, aren't you?" she asked, ingenuously brightening up her smile.

I wasn't in the mood for niceties. I removed my plastic Federation card from my wallet and presented it to her. "I think I'm a teacher," I said sarcastically. "At least . . . I think that's what it says on my card."

"I've always wanted to be a teacher," she continued, with a pretentious, almost commercial civility. "I just love little kids. Youth is so much fun and so exciting...teaching must be so rewarding. Tell me, what are your pupils like?"

I paused for a long time. "Well," I said, "let me see. I have shy kids ... aggressive kids ... kids that need prodding ... kids that balk if pushed ... kids susceptible to colds ... kids that never get sick ... kids who aren't interested in playing music ... kids who will bang out a tune on anything ... black kids, white kids, mulatto kids, Spanish kids, Italian kids, West Indian kids, wasp kids, Catholic kids, kids from South America, kids from Nova Scotia ... kids that had polio ... kids that have sickle cell anemia ... kids that have cold sores and hangnails ... one kid who had a nervous breakdown at seven ... kids who have scars from beatings ... kids whose parents never discipline them ... kids who wear tattered clothes ... kids who wear the latest disco fashions ... kids who love me ... kids who think I screw the teacher down the hall ... kids that frown all the time ... kids that never stop smiling...."

I stopped. The woman stared at me as if I were crazy. I probably was crazy. After a few moments of silence the woman reached over and touched my arm and sensuously planted a fuchsia-coloured kiss on the nape of my neck. "I'm curious," she said, stroking my arm. "Do you really screw the teacher down the hall?"

Tuesday, May 1

I was surprised when the Mayor's secretary phoned me today and asked me to participate in a special session at City Hall involving a council that had been set up to help relieve the tension in the Jane-Finch Corridor.

Speaking through a stiff headcold, I told the council, using my experiences as ammunition, that schools must do more to meet the needs of poor kids. I said it was a moral concern. Everybody nodded in agreement.

Thursday, May 3

Upset with his son's progress report, Mr. Corelli called me at the school and requested an interview. Because he worked the late afternoon shift at a glass and paint factory, he was unable to come to the school during regular hours. I told him I'd be glad to drop by his place on Sunday afternoon.

I knocked on the door of the tiny brick townhouse shortly after twelve. A thin wiry man in a sleeveless white tee-shirt answered the door.

"I'm Frank's dad," he said, motioning me inside, offering me the lazy-boy armchair that dominated the tiny living room. I found myself facing about a dozen bowling trophies crowded together on top of a rusty filing cabinet. Portraits of John and Robert Kennedy, painted on black felt, hung above the window.

"As you can see, we're beer drinkers here!" and he pointed to the hall. I saw it was completely papered in Labatt's "50" beer bottle labels. "My wife did that," he proclaimed proudly. "Took her six months. If you can find even a speck of space between the labels, I'll give you a twelve-pack free!"

He brought me a beer, slumped down in the sofa and groaned. "Frank ain't been doin so good in school . . . has he?" he finally asked.

"No . . . not exactly," I replied, pushing back on the arms of the lazy-boy, trying to get comfortable.

"Do you think Frank's gonna pass?"

"I don't believe in failing pupils."

"But is he tryin?" he snapped.

"I think it takes Frank a lot to get himself motivated," I hedged, uncertain of exactly what to say.

"Look," Mr. Corelli said matter-of-factly, as he smoothed back the black tufts of this thinning hair, "tomorrow I think I'll show up in your class and give him a few belts."

I was shocked. "You mean in front of the class?"

"I give him lickins at home, but it don't do no good," he

replied, shaking his head. "Maybe in front of his friends—"

"That's out of the question! You can't teach a kid anything through violence or humiliating punishment. I can't stop you from punishing your son at home, Mr. Corelli, but I would never allow him to be hit at school. Not under any circumstances." I was trying to control my anger.

"Well then," he said calmly, "*you* give it to him in front of the kids, if you don't want me to."

My face felt hot, and I laughed nervously. "No way, Mr. Corelli! Let's talk about the problem first, and maybe we can come up with some solution."

Head tilted, a sombre expression on his face, Mr. Corelli then fired questions at me in swift progression, ranging from the "too lenient" disciplinary approach of most teachers to the high cost of school taxes. Eventually he got around to what was really bothering him.

"It's hard copin with Frank and bein alone. Ever since his mother walked out on me it's been hell. She went out to the Becker's store one day and never come back. I know Frank blames me, cause we used to fight so much."

After we finished talking, I recommended a social agency I thought might help.

I placed Frank in an individualized program consisting mostly of arts and craft-oriented activities, and tried not to pressure him on his academic subjects, at the same time searching for a tool I could use.

Previously, I'd tried to put Frank in a special reading series, but he went through the readers perfunctorily. Then I remembered his dad mentioning Frank's comic book collection, and I asked him to bring some in. We went over the comic books together, and soon Frank's working vocabulary jumped.

Monday, May 7

From a distance I could see Lambchops, the current grade six bully, standing at the end of the hall. He hitched up his pants, lifted his shoulders and snapped his fingers. Responding to his signal, three kids suddenly ran out of the washroom and pounced on a kid whom Lambchops had seen walking by. "Kick his fuckin head in," one of them cried.

I arrived on the scene seconds later. The kids took off like a shot, while the victim was left to nurse a split lip and a few bruises.

"It was only a joke," the kid whined when I questioned him. His eyes searched mine, sad and pleading. "Don't do anything, please! They'll only get me on the way home."

Friday, May 11

Orantes, nine, swaggered over to my desk. "You got any hair on your chest?" It wasn't the kind of question I expected to be asked. "Sir," Orantes continued, "you ain't got no hair on your chest. My daddy gots lots of hair on his."

"You're wrong, Orantes. I do happen to have some hair on my chest," I replied, with a mixture of embarrassment and pride. "Most men do. But I'm sure your dad has more than anybody else."

"Lemme see then!" was the immediate shouted response. I had been trapped, out-foxed. "Lemme see! Undo your shirt and lemme have a look!"

I tried to gracefully ease myself out by saying, "Take my word for it, Orantes. Your dad has lots of hair on his chest. I don't have very much. Your dad wins!"

"You gots more hair on your head," he continued undaunted, "but my dad gots more on his chest. He looks like a hairy gorilla!"

"I'm sure your dad looks much more like a gorilla than I do, Orantes. And I really don't have any hair on my chest, either. I was just kidding."

"Show me then," he demanded at once. I had been sucked right in. "Show me right now! Prove you ain't got no hair!"

I gave up. I opened my shirt a little and pulled down the

neckline of my tee-shirt, revealing a few blond tufts. "See! I've just got a few—not like your dad. Okay?"

But Orantes had more up his sleeve. "My dad's gots a cock this big!" he went on, holding his hand a good two feet apart.

"Subject dropped!" I barked.

Monday, May 14

Fred warned me he wouldn't be around next September. He was taking a year's sabbatical to study in England. He figured he'd probably be placed in a new school on his return. It was Board policy to move a principal to a new school every five years. He offered me a job on his new staff if I ever wanted to join him.

"Would you like to be principal of a nice middle-class school?" I asked.

"Not really. And even if I did, the Board would stick me in another inner-city school anyway. Once you've been successful as an inner-city school principal, they always place you in another one. That's their idea of a reward."

Wednesday, May 16

It was one of the first warm days after the long winter. After class I decided to soak up some sun on a park bench near the school. The air smelled fresh and the sun felt good on my face. I lit my pipe and started marking a batch of exercise books I had brought along.

Shortly afterwards I was approached by three black kids—two boys and a girl—about ten years old. They wore identical shiny nylon jackets, tight-fitting jeans and orange fluorescent sneakers. I didn't recognize them as students from the school.

As soon as the girl caught my eyes she flashed a wide smile and started snapping her fingers. The two boys also joined in, finger-snapping and slowly rocking back and forth. Weaving gracefully in my direction, they stopped only a few feet from where I was sitting and began a rhythmic cooing that sent a tingle up my spine. Then the girl began to strut and sashay, moving faster, her companions following. I put down my book and drew heavily on my pipe, swaddled by the soft beauty of their voices, and mesmerized by the fluid movements of their bodies that shifted effortlessly from one intricate pattern to another.

Suddenly the girl's arms shot up and the voices and dancing stopped. They stood there motionless, hands on their hips. After a few seconds, blissful smiles drooped into frowns. I reached into my pocket, pulled out some change, and handed it to the girl—a small price for the pleasure they had given to me. Wide smiles blossomed once again. Then they turned and headed back towards the street.

Thursday, May 17

I stayed at the school late last night, setting up a reading clinic in my class. I had learned about this new approach to teaching language skills at a recent workshop.

At one end of the room I equipped a large rectangular table with a record player and a dozen headphones. In the other corner I set up a language master and two filmstrip projectors so the kids could watch cartoon strips of classic fairy tales.

My pièce de resistance was an eight-track cassette machine complete with tapes of exciting children's stories. I recorded the stories myself, and my voice was still hoarse from reading aloud about ten Dr. Seuss books.

Whenever I stayed late at the school, I usually spent the night at my parents' house, just a couple of miles outside the Corridor.

That night, for some reason, I woke up about four o'clock in the morning, and couldn't get back to sleep. Rather than toss and turn, I decided to go for a drive.

Almost instinctively, I headed back to the Corridor. I parked my van in the school lot and sat on the street curb across from the school.

For a long time, I just sat staring at the school in the pre-dawn light, thinking of all the events that had gone on behind those drab, brown walls. From the outside, the building looked just like any other school; it was hard to imagine all the lost and troubled souls that passed through those doors each day.

One by one, people emerged bleary-eyed from the nearby buildings, clutching lunch pails or brown bags, heading towards the bus stops. A drizzle of rain began to fall.

I sat in the rain watching the Italian labourers in heavy shirts and trousers of thick fabric, West Indian workers in woollen caps, some carrying transistor radios the size of small suitcases. One black woman lifted her skirt and whirled in a little dance. Another woman in a colourful print shawl looked up into the sky, inviting the rain to cool her face.

The whole area looked so bleak, so sterile, yet strangely at peace. The grey high-rises seemed aloof, almost stoic in the soft mist that was forming. I listened to the steady rumble of trucks down the nearby industrial streets, birds chirping on the telephone wires, the screech of the garbage trucks pulling up to the backs of the buildings. Everything seemed so integral, even purposeful. But I knew that behind the faceless concrete facades, families were awakening to a new day of troubles . . . hustling to survive . . . or just giving in to despair.

I needed a wake-up coffee before the school day began. I headed over to the local plaza.

Friday, May 18

This morning John decided I should purify my blood. He sent a strange drink up to my class, which he claimed would do the trick. Made of vinegar, water and honey, and perhaps several other unidentified things, it smelled awful.

Phil watched me taste it, and then remarked: "Jeez, sir, you're just like my dad. He needs his shot first thing in the mornin too!"

Sunday, May 20

On Sunday, I went down to the boardwalk for a walk along the lake, just to think. As I strolled along, hands in my pockets, head down, the planks in the boardwalk seemed like measured steps in an uphill climb to sanity. I was mentally measuring my fitness for another year in the classroom. Was I up to it? The thought of teaching for another year made me feel that I was trapped in a dungeon, losing all count of time. The warden might be a nice guy and the food not bad, but I was suffocating—I had to get out. I'd put in my time.

I decided to quit. I took a deep breath and started for home.

Jenny was sitting in the living room. When I told her she looked at me intently. "I know. I sensed it."

"Well? How do you feel about it?"

"I feel you'll be an old man by the time you're thirty-five if you keep on the way you're going. You know I'm behind you . . . and the kids will still be there."

Tuesday, May 22

I couldn't sleep last night; my mind was flooded with doubts. Did it really make any difference, my being there? Am I copping out, running away? And so on and so on. . . .

I hated to tell Fred; I felt I was betraying him. When I finally got up the nerve, he took it well, understanding my position.

"Sure, Peter, I'll sign your leave of absence papers, only because I know you'll change your mind."

Wednesday, May 23

After lunch, Mickey told me he had tried to take a bite out of his townhouse. He showed me a chipped tooth and bleeding gums to prove it.

Thursday, May 24

Okay class! Take your seats please! Mickey, will you please put down your chair!

But you said for us to take our seats!

Mickey's a smartass! Why don't you hit him!

Shut your face! You're dead!

Okay, now settle down! We're going to talk about last night's election results. Who knows who the new Prime Minister of Canada is?

Joe Clark! Joe Clark!

Right! Who knows what party he belongs to?

Whiskey! He drinks whiskey at parties!

No way, turkey! He drinks what my dad drinks—Molson's Golden!

Joe Clark don't likes black people!

Who said that?

My mom! She told me he don't like black skin.

Trudle likes Chinese people—that's why he gots slanty eyes!

So what! He's got skinny hair; Joe Clark ain't bald.

Joe Clark ain't gots no brains!

He looks like a retard! His chin fell off cause he talks too much!

Okay. Open your notebooks, class, and let's write this down. "Joe Clark is the new Prime Minister of Canada. Pierre Trudeau is the Leader of the Opposition."

Trudle's the guy with the crazy wife with big tits. The Prince of England looks down her dress—my mom read it in a magazine.

Friday, May 25

Duke, my wild and unruly former student, liked to return periodically for a talk. He had quit school after junior-high. When he was in my class, he often wore a button: "Sure I raise hell. So what?"

Out in the parking lot, he showed me the new paint job on his motorcycle. Like always, he wore faded jeans, a wrinkled tee-shirt, and a leather jacket. A fat friend was kneeling beside Duke's bike, checking the engine. Painted on the deep-blue gas tank was a picture of the earth and a distant star, with a bright beam of white light shooting from the star towards the earth. The words "The King Is Coming" were stencilled in gold letters over the picture. Running down the back fender were the fluorescent-green words "Bikers for the Lord."

"Remember when I got Lindsay to eat that dog shit, after shoving a kleenex full a snot in his mouth?"

"Do I!"

"Well," he said, leaning against his bike, "I didn't really mean it. I don't do things like that no more. I've changed."

Monday, May 28

I was saddened to hear John was thinking of retiring next year. He was hoping to do what he had always dreamed of: raise vegetables. He planned on buying a farmhouse on prime agricultural land down in the Niagara Peninsula. "With the fantastic compost heap I intend to create, I'm going to raise the finest vegetables in the country!"

I was going to miss John.

Wednesday, May 30

I visited the group home where Barry lives. It had been two years since he left my class, and I decided to see how he was doing.

A teenage girl, both of whose arms were wrapped in gauze from fingertips to armpits, opened the door for me. She was bandaged to prevent her from hurting herself: she bit spoon-sized chunks from her arms with her own teeth. One side of her head was a mass of black scabs, with a few remaining tufts of hair sticking out. Barry, she told me, was out on a camping trip.

It was hard to handle. Next time, I'll phone first and meet Barry in a restaurant.

Friday, June 1

One of Mickey's older brothers had just been released from jail, and Mickey was pretty excited about it. All day long, he drew pictures of the event. One picture showed his brother being led away from jail by a giant creature.

"What's that thing with your brother?" I asked.

"Don't you know who *that* is?" Jessie asked, a puzzled grin breaking across his face as he leaned across to Mickey's desk.

"Not really. Who is it, Mickey?"

"It's the Amazing Hulk! *He saved my brother!* Didn't you know that? He sprang Tommy from jail!"

When I picked up my mail at the office, I got a great lift—I'd been given the HAID award of the year!

Monday, June 4

Last March, Fred invited several art therapists to speak to the staff on the benefits of "spontaneous art" for inner-city children. A recently published research paper, demonstrating that kids who had difficulty talking about their anxieties often had remarkable success drawing pictures of what was troubling them, caught his interest.

After listening to the art therapists describe their program, the staff agreed to hire one for a probationary period, with the option of extending the program if it was successful.

We were each asked to submit the name of one student who might benefit. Although I felt I had many kids who could be helped by the program, I decided to put Mickey's name on the list. Many weary hours I had spent trying to help him talk out his problems, but he was still seething with bottled-up anger. He needed help fast.

Each week Anthony, his therapist, would withdraw Mickey from class and take him down to a corner of the students' lunch room. Under his expert guidance, Mickey was encouraged to express himself with crayons, paint and clay. He responded by painting pictures of army tanks in battle and, later, of his house and family.

Anthony also encouraged him to talk about his paintings. After the first month, Mickey was able to open up to him and talk freely, and soon a good relationship grew between them.

While following Mickey's progress through weekly meetings with Anthony, I began to know the therapist as a person, and was impressed. He explained that art therapy had its theoretical roots in the psychoanalytic work of Sigmund Freud, utilizing his theories of the anal, oral and genital personalities. As he analyzed Mickey's drawings within this framework, I became fascinated.

"Mickey didn't even have to draw a thing before I knew he was a combination of oral and anal personality development," Anthony told me the first time we spoke about Mickey.

"Really?"

"Because the first thing he said to me was 'Eat shit!' "

But the staff eventually decided that not enough kids were receiving help; teachers could send only one student per class. And although we all agreed the therapy was beneficial, some teachers wondered whether more kids would be helped if the money was spent instead on school supplies. So the art therapy program died. The option was not picked up; there was simply not enough support for it.

When Mickey had to say goodbye to Anthony, he became extremely upset. Anthony was one person he'd become attached to. Now his behaviour began to revert, and it was as if nothing had happened at all.

Wednesday, June 6

Suzanne stormed into the staff room while I was eating lunch—"I just went home for lunch and the super in my buildin kicked us out! He changed the lock on our door so's we can't get back in! I couldn't even get my sweater!"

I offered her some of my lunch and she eagerly sat down beside me. "Why did your super kick you out?" I asked.

"He says my mom's a welfare bum and can't pay the rent. But mom's already paid! She just gots a new job! And he threw out my baby sister and her babysitter and says we're good-for-nothin niggers! My mom's gonna go to court cause she's real mad and she don't even know where we're gonna stay tonight."

I thought only for a moment. "Tell your mom you can stay with me." She smiled and threw her arms around my neck.

After speaking to her mom, Suzanne told me they would be staying with a neighbour on another floor in their building, but she thanked me for the offer. For the next two days her mother went to court, trying to settle the problem. She got her apartment back, but because of the days she took off to appear in court, she lost her new job.

Thursday, June 7

At nine o'clock, I assembled the kids on the carpet. "Well, boys and girls, does anybody have any news?" I asked, as I did first thing every morning.

Two kids immediately leaped up, as if the law of gravity had been temporarily suspended. Esther Anne was one of them. I was surprised she volunteered; she seldom spoke, even when asked. For her to volunteer news was something stupendous.

"Me first! Me first!" Georgette howled suddenly. She jumped up, waving her arms wildly. "Me first! I'm before Esther Anne! You promised!"

She was right. "I'll be right with you, Esther Anne, but I already promised Georgette that she could be the first today to give the news."

I was pretty impatient as Georgette described her sister's birthday party. Esther Anne was on my mind, and I was eager to hear what news she had to report.

When Georgette finished, I turned to Esther Anne. She stared at me for a moment, her burning eyes darting from my face to the floor. "I changed my mind," she said at last. "I ain't got no news today."

I was disappointed, but tried to be positive. "Okay, Esther Anne. Maybe you'll have some news tomorrow. . . ."

At the end of the day, she came up to me as I was packing up. "Sir, do you wants to know what my news was?"

At last! "Why I sure do," I answered eagerly, happy at the chance to draw her out of her shell.

"Well . . ." she began, slowly, "my mom, she burned me with a cigarette yesterday."

"Where?"

"Right here . . . and here . . . and here," she replied, pointing to her neck, hand and forearm.

Friday, June 8

Carmen and Sasha were delightful children. In other schools they may have been labelled "slow learners" or "behaviour problems," but I thought they were great. At the end of a long day, it was always a joy when they volunteered to stay after class and help me tidy up.

This afternoon, while they were helping me clean out the cupboard, I casually remarked that kids today don't seem to really try to get along with each other.

"How you expect them to get along with other folks," replied Sasha, "when they don't even like the person that they are?"

So much has been thought and said, planned and researched, felt and imagined about poor kids. Even though they didn't have a Masters in Education, little Carmen and Sasha hit on the cornerstone of the approach I had long ago decided on. Self-respect is the beginning.

Monday, June 11

During the last weeks of school, I took the kids to the park almost daily. I brought a cassette machine along with some tapes of old blues artists—listening to the blues has always had a peaceful effect on me, and I hoped the kids could relax to some of the songs.

The first day I took along the cassette machine, I put it under a tree and turned it on. A half dozen kids started tapping their feet almost immediately to the beat as Bessie Smith, Charlie Patton, Blind Lemon Jefferson and Billie Holiday sang haunting parables about the tragi-comic underbelly of urban life, as if the words were torn from their souls.

Kids who weren't interested in the music ran across the park to the baseball diamond or made for the swings. I lay down on the park bench and watched a sky full of dark clouds move slowly overhead, as if they were slowed in passing by the beauty of the music. A brisk gust of wind scattered paper and debris; the leaves flicked and eddied about the bench.

Mickey inched up to me and nudged my arm. "The music sounds real good," he said. "But it's sad."

Birds fluttered in the tops of nearby trees. A group of

kids, groaning, puffing, and wet with sweat tried to grab onto a large overhanging branch on one of the large trees. Finally, after many failed attempts, Lance dragged over a trash can and tipped it upside down. The kids propped the can against the tree and used it to boost themselves up.

Samantha sat down in the dirt in front of me. She stared for a few minutes across the field, her eyes scanning the rows of high-rise apartments that loomed on the outer edges of the park. They resembled giant gravestones under the low, menacing sky.

"You wanna know somethin, sir," she said wistfully, still staring into the distance. "We used to live right downtown in this rotten place called Regent's Park. Then my mom said, 'We're gonna move to the suburbs.' Now that we're here we gots more people callin us names and beatin us up more than before. I thought the suburbs was supposed to be a nice place. Now I wanna go back downtown."

I put my arm around her shoulder and watched a tiny figure making its way from the schoolyard across the field to the park. As the figure grew closer I realized it was Priscilla, who had been absent during the morning. She ran the last few yards up to my bench, a sweet smile wrinkling her face.

"I'm the best kid in the class now, sir!" she announced triumphantly.

"No you're not!" Samantha snapped and impulsively kissed me on the cheek. "I am!"

Priscilla placed her hands on her hips and looked up at the sky. "I gots baptized last night—so there! Hallelulia and praise the Lord!"

"Congratulations, Priscilla," I said.

"I went to a healin meetin, too," she continued, a tumult of emotions. "This man touched people on the head and the Holy Spirit knocked them out. There was this fat lady there, and the man with the Spirit touched her and turned her skinny. I saw it! Her shoes was so big they didn't fit her no more! Then the man cured my brother's sickle cell blood. Praise the Lord!"

"I don't believe you!" Mickey broke in viciously. "You're a liar!"

"Shut your face!" Priscilla snapped back.

Vinnie came running up to the bench, arms pumping and face sweat-streaked. He sat down heavily beside Priscilla, trying clumsily to fasten his sneakers.

"God praise you Vinnie!" cried Priscilla.

Vinnie looked stunned. "What?"

"I gots the spirit, Vinnie!" she cried, grinning widely.

Vinnie stopped struggling with his shoelaces and sat still. "There's no such thing as spirits!" he declared. "The guy in our buildin everybody says is a boogey man, he's jus an ole drunk."

Priscilla was annoyed. "I'm not talkin about boogey men. I mean God's spirit. I gots religion!"

Mickey scowled and muttered, "You're crazy!" and ran across to the tree where kids were starting to climb down. Then he pulled away the trash can just as Pasquale was about to descend. Pasquale dropped from the tree onto the ground, landing with a loud thud—and a curse. Priscilla watched the event with growing distain. "You needs the spirit!" she shouted. Mickey raised his fist in a mock salute. "Up yours!"

Tuesday, June 12

Usually, if you have to hide out, the bathroom is the place to do it. At least you're assured privacy in the toilet, if nowhere else. And that was why I began hiding out in the staff washroom during recess, trying to get the peace and quiet I needed to finish off some paperwork.

During recess this afternoon I was sitting on the throne marking papers, when I heard the door to the washroom open. I froze.

A pair of red sneakers appeared suddenly under the door of my hideaway cubicle. Just as suddenly the sneakers disappeared, only to be replaced by a pair of knees, then two hands, and then Mickey's head thrust under the door, grinning up at me.

"Havin a nice shit, sir?"

Wednesday, June 13

Mickey's teenage sister showed up at my door, Mickey standing behind her, crying. He had been beaten up on the way to school, she explained, and had returned home in tears. So she decided to walk him to school.

As soon as Mickey entered the room, he started screaming. "T.J.'s going to kill fuckin Leroy," he shouted. "He's gonna punch him out for beatin me up!" He wailed, blinking away tears, and flailing his arms as if at an invisible adversary.

I drew him close to me, and it was the only time he didn't push me away. While I wiped the tears from his eyes, I began rubbing his back slowly, rhythmically. His tight little face began to relax as I stroked his damp forehead soothingly and told him to take a deep breath. He sighed, and slowly the frenzy melted away. His shoulders loosened, then he crawled up on my lap and fell asleep.

Oddly enough, my kids just went on quietly with their work, and no one disturbed us.

Thursday, June 14

I took the class to Ontario Place as an end of the year outing. Most of the kids had never been there, although they had heard stories about the fantastic playground and the giant water slide. Because of the budget cuts I wasn't able to reserve a school bus, so we had to travel by public transportation. Several parent volunteers came along to help me with the kids.

Except for a skuffle between Mickey and Vinnie over who was going to sit at the very back of the bus, the kids were reasonably well-behaved. The bus let us off at Exhibition

Stadium, and we walked the rest of the way to Ontario Place, a short stroll.

Once inside, the kids exploded everywhere and it took about half an hour to round them up.

We saw a short film about Ontario that was playing at Cinesphere, a theatre with a giant, curved screen. At the beginning of the film the Premier of Ontario, Bill Davis, appeared on the screen, mouthing homilies about the greatness of the province.

"Hey ... lookit him!" Mickey blurted. "It's Al Capone!"

"Yahoo," Vinnie exclaimed, "a real gangster!"

"He ain't no hood!" Samantha cried. "He's a millionaire. Lookit his clothes!"

"So what if he's rich!" Priscilla bellowed, "who wants to get dressed up like that all the time!"

I hushed the kids, explaining to them that other people were trying to watch the film, and that they had to behave if they wanted to go to the playground.

"He's bribin us again," Mickey laughed. But they did settle down for the remainder of the film.

After the film the kids complained that they were hungry, so we ate lunch by the water, outside the entrance to the theatre. Vinnie started throwing rocks at the swans and was joined by several other kids. I moved the class to the middle of an open area.

After lunch we marched over to the adventure playground, full of activities to enjoy: rope forts, climbers of every shape and description, teeter-totters, pulley rides, tunnels and slides. Most of the kids wanted to go on the water slide, but couldn't afford the two dollar charge.

"Everywhere kids go they gotta pay money for the most fun thing!" Priscilla complained. She kicked the fence outside the water slide, and watched the kids who could afford it laugh deliriously as they sailed down the giant curving slide, landing in various positions in the pool below. Most of the other kids forgot about the slide and amused themselves with other things. But Priscilla stood staring at the water slide for a long time.

After several hours of horsing around, we left. Samantha threw up all over my lap on the bus ride home, much to my wife's disgust when I arrived at my front door.

Friday, June 15
When I found out the local junior-high was putting on a year-end variety show, I decided to go. Maybe I'd see some of my old kids.

Sure enough, several showed up. The first performer, in fact, was none other than Buddy. Even though he hadn't officially been one of my students, he was still one of the family—sort of.

Buddy was part of a dancing troupe, which did a beautifully choreographed disco set to the background of a Thelma Huston song. He was dressed in patchwork quilt knickers, striped suspenders and platinum-coloured satin shirt, his former mountain of Afro hair now neatly dreadlocked. The name of his group was "Fight the Power!"

The performance ended with some teenage girls reading an essay called "The Black Manifesto," aimed at getting the black community organized in fighting racism.

After the show, Buddy and I had a friendly chat. It's funny how much affection I had for this character who gave me so many rough moments. He told me he didn't hang out anymore with his old friends, most of his buddies were older and "into heavier things, man." He was seriously taking up boxing, "and if I ever get to be Champ, I'll mention your name to the TV guys."

Monday, June 18
This evening after dinner, I decided to drop by Mickey's house to make my farewells. I especially wanted to thank his

mom for all the lunches she prepared for me during the two years I taught T.J. and Mickey.

T.J. greeted me at the door with a beer in his hand. He looked drunk. Sandra, their eighteen-year-old sister, was sitting with her mother on the sofa talking to some of her friends. When she saw me, she turned and waved hello, her pink terrycloth robe and slippers, with what looked like kitty fluff around the ankles, making quite a picture. Except for two drooping ringlets, her hair was pinned back by a pink taffeta ribbon.

She looked troubled, her face puffy, and even from across the room I could see the wrinkles in her forehead. But there was also something different about her face, something I couldn't put my finger on.

Suddenly it hit me. Her teeth, previously grungy with decay and mottled with tobacco stains, now appeared thoroughly bright and shiny! They looked marvellous, and I couldn't figure it out. While I was standing there, little Mickey came over—he was wearing pajamas—and handed me half a mickey of rye.

"Did you see my sister's new teeth?" he asked. "She just got them yesterday." Of course—Sandra's new teeth were false!

I stayed about an hour, until everyone around me was hopelessly drunk, except Mickey. I couldn't handle watching T.J. wobble from one room to the next, so I thanked them for their hospitality, and left for home.

Tuesday, June 19

This world is dumb! A man on the TV said a piece of a spaceship is gonna fall on our heads!

Hey, gimmie back my pencil!

Yes, Vinnie, I agree. The world really does seem dumb sometimes.

It's my pencil! I found it on the floor!

Sir! Wasn't Elvis the best?

He was pretty good. I liked him.

See! I told you! White people are the best singers!

Hey, I didn't say white people were the best singers.

There are good black singers as well as white singers.

Liar! You just said Elvis was the best!

Brown people can sing good, too!

My aunt put my little cousin in the dryer last night. He lost five dollars at the store so my aunt put him in the dryer and he went round and round.

Is that true, Mickey?

Wipe your nose Georgette! It's full of snot!

Welfare face!

It's true! I saw it!

Don't eat it! Mr. McLaren! Georgette's licking off her snot!

You looks just like my dad, sir. Exceptin my dad's black.

My friend said I look like Elvis.

I look like Debbie Boone then!

Yuck! I hates Debbie Boone! She's gots pimples.

You . . . you light up my life . . .

Shutup your stupid singin!

You gots an awful voice, Samantha.

My mom threw a wooden spoon at me this mornin.

What happened?

It missed. That's all.

I was at the creek last night, Mr. McLaren. I saw these teenagers with their pants down.

Wait a minute. Mickey wants to tell me about his cousin and Vinnie wants to tell me about his mother.

I don't wanna talk no more about my mother.

Take your finger out of your zipper!

Awww! I thought it was his cock stickin out!

Mr. McLaren! Georgette's nose is all green again from snot. There's a little green worm comin out of her nose!

You . . . you light up my life . . . light up my life . . .

Shaddup! You sound welfare!

My mom told me I look just like Harry Belafonte.

He's an old man, stupid. I seen him on a record. My mom says he's an oreo cookie—black on the outside and white in the middle.

What does that mean?

I dunno. He tastes good.

Haaaaaaaaaa!

I gots a new mom. She's deaf.

She's a mental!

No she ain't! She just can't hear.

You ain't nothin but a hound dog . . .

Shaddup! You ain't no good either!

Is the sky really gonna fall, Mr. McLaren?

Probably the bits from the space station will land in the ocean.

I hope it lands on Vinnie's balls.

Wednesday, June 20

On our daily walk to the park, everything was going smoothly until little Carlos, a moment before happy and cheerful, suddenly fell to the ground, weeping uncontrollably.

"I miss my mom! My *real* mom!" he cried out to me.

"Your real mom? Where is she?" I asked, as I picked him up in my arms to comfort him.

"She's in New Brunswick," he whimpered. "My dad's sendin me on the train to see her in July and they're gettin a divorce!"

I tried to cheer him up by saying, "Why that's only a few weeks away, all you have to do is wait awhile."

But he continued to sob. "But my dad's getting divorced now from my other mom so that means I'm gonna have three moms!"

I had no idea what to say, trying to sort out which mom he meant when, as suddenly as he began to cry, he jumped up, wiped away his tears and headed over to a bunch of kids playing soccer.

Thursday, June 21

Guy taught English to new Canadians who could barely understand a word of what was being said to them. He was a valuable resource. Every day he withdrew three or four kids from each class, and in unique ways taught them to speak English: he took them to supermarkets and had them read the food labels; he showed them places like the Kensington Market and other ethnic communities that radiated different atmospheres.

I didn't really get to know Guy until recently, when we had a chat in the staff room. He had just finished a frustrating interview with the father of one of his students and looked exhausted.

"I finally met the father of one of my kids . . . finally," he began. "For the last two months, Wally has been telling me, 'My daddy's gone away! My daddy's gone away again!' I didn't know if he was a travelling salesman, or what.

"Well, his dad just showed up, and we had a long talk. It turns out he's a mercenary, he hires himself out to fight in wars all over the world. He just came back from a campaign in Arabia, where he said it had been 'particularly gory'— that's all he'd tell me, just that it was a 'private war.' Now he's decided to take an interest in his kid. I told him that Wally missed him when he was away, and he just looked at me and said, 'What can I do? It's my job.'"

Guy and I compared notes and found we had much in common; our teaching philosophies were very similar. He was a bit worried that Fred hadn't come around to see what he was doing—he didn't know whether that meant Fred thought he was doing a good job, or whether he simply wasn't interested. "The only time he's ever come into my room," Guy remarked, "was to get a light for his cigar."

I explained that it was Fred's philosophy not to go into a teacher's room until the end of the semester, unless he was invited.

Guy had been hired on a short-term basis in January, so he was on the teachers' surplus list. Although he had ten years' experience teaching with the Toronto Board, he had only been with North York for a short while, and the Board does not consider work done for other Boards to count when compiling the seniority list.

He received his pink slip and has decided to go into the travel agent business.

Friday, June 22

As I was walking through the parking lot at lunch I met Duke on his "Bikers for the Lord" motorcycle. His tee-shirt read, "A message to all you virgins: Thanks for nothin!" Straddling the back of the seat was a young girl about twelve, on the back of her windbreaker a fluorescent slogan: "Save a Mouse—Eat a Pussy."

"This is Mary Lynn," Duke announced. "I'm workin on savin her soul."

I smiled and shook her hand.

Duke cleared his throat and reached into his pocket. "This note's from my mom. She heard you was leavin the school. Whatever she says goes for me, too."

Then Duke and his girlfriend put on their helmets and raised their fists in a salute. "You're one of the decent ones!" Duke yelled, revving up the engine. "So long, sir!" he cried, pulling one last dramatic "wheelie" and waving goodbye. It reminded me of a scene from the old Lone Ranger television series when the Lone Ranger reared on his white horse and waved into the camera.

I opened the note.

"When Duke told me you were leaving teaching to go back to school, I felt I had to write you a note. I hope you will always work with children in some way. I would like every child to have at least one teacher like you. You make learning fun, but still learning. Thanks for all you've done for Duke."

It was rare for a parent to say thank you. Not that they weren't often grateful, but many found it difficult to communicate their feelings openly.

I put the note in my wallet and headed off towards the restaurant, the smoke from Duke's bike still lingering in the parking lot.

Monday, June 25

There was only one day of school left before the summer holidays. I earlier had sent home a note with each kid, reminding the parents not to forget to send some cookies or cakes or other treats for our party.

Kim arrived this morning looking depressed. "My mom won't give me nothin to bring," she said, wiping away tears. "She says she's savin all our money to move out of this crappy neighbourhood."

Liz invited my class to her room to share some of the fun of the final party of the year. She put a disco album on, and started dancing with the kids. "Let's *really* give them something to talk about," she said to me, grinning. She stuck out her hip my way, and for the next few songs we did "the bump." Our hips bounced and we twirled round and round, much to the delight of the kids.

To our surprise, there were no lewd remarks or obscene gestures. Some of the kids had tears in their eyes; others couldn't wait to get out the door.

Tuesday, June 26

On the last day of school, Samantha left a note on my desk.

This is only for you to read no one els but you.

Dear Sir. I have something to tell you. I want to tell you that I love you I not only love you because you are my teacher. I love you and I'm respecte. I love you like a father not just because you techer. But I wich that I had the hart to tell you I love you other than write this letter.
  P.S.
                    Yours truly
                    From Samantha

Epilogue

In July I had lunch with Fran, a woman who had taught me at Teacher's College. We hadn't seen each other for quite a while but, as always, there was an immediate rapport between us.

When I told her of my decision to go back to school, she looked anxious, almost apologetic. She admitted nothing much had been said about the plight of kids like mine during the years I'd been at Teacher's College "... but we're working on it."

"Working on it! That's not good enough!" I suddenly felt very uncomfortable—from her point of view, what right did I have to be sounding off? I'd opted out...."Sorry Fran. I get so wound up about the whole mess ... I guess what I actually want is a complete restructuring of society. Despite everything, I suppose I'm just as idealistic as ever.... No! That's not true! I *have* tried to be practical. For instance, there's nothing biological in, say, a West Indian kid's low performance—the problem is strictly social. The school system just doesn't provide the tools we need to help these kids adjust. Maybe if I'd had only eight or ten kids to work with...."

"Come on, Peter, be realistic! That costs money and cut-backs in education money isn't exactly news."

"Okay, okay, but believe me—if something doesn't start changing, we're in for trouble—you can't deny that."

Fran threw up her hands. "Let's assume I agree with you. Now let's look at it from another direction. Lots of people aren't choosing to have children these days—right? So don't you think it's unreasonable to expect them to pay for all the things you want for other people's kids?"

"Well, they'll end up paying anyway—social services, subsidized housing, welfare money, retraining—you name it. The cost of providing more teachers is about equal to the cost of building a few miles of highway. Surely kids are more important than highways?" I took a sip of my wine, wondering how I could make my point. "Let me put it this way, then. Imagine you're a little Jamaican girl. You and your mother and two brothers have just arrived from Jamaica, leaving your father behind. Your mother has a grade five education and lands a factory job. You live in a subsidized high-rise; your white neighbours hate you because your mother has taken away one of *their* jobs. At school the other kids call you names and make fun of the way you talk, and your teacher can hardly make out what you're saying. Your brothers get in fights trying to protect you, etc., etc., etc. And that builds a good self-image? Now, do you think you'd have the guts to hang in there and be a good little student? More likely you'll quit as soon as you're old enough and be lucky to get some crummy job—that is, if you're not knocked-up first!"

Fran, looking annoyed, sat silent for a few moments, her face closed in. "Even if I agree with what you're saying, you have to admit that kids today have never had it so good compared to the past."

"Kids *are* better off today. But there are parts of our cities where kids are hungry and abused, and it's on the rise—you read the newspapers. I've spent almost three years with these kids!" I was getting hot. It must seem to Fran that I'm attacking *her*. "Listen," I said, lowering my voice, "I'm not blaming you, Fran."

"Well . . . maybe I am partly to blame. At least in not preparing teachers for what they're going to find in some of the inner-city schools. Maybe I should get out there in the world and see what's going on." She took my hand and squeezed it.

I took a deep breath. "Fran, I'm so damn frightened for the kids. If they're headed for self-destruction and violence, then the schools and governments, everybody, must accept part of the blame. We're spending millions on the energy crisis, but our greatest resource isn't oil . . . it's kids!"

"You never used to sound like this in Teacher's College, Peter."

"Maybe I should have, but how could I? I was an

innocent then. . . . Teachers like me can rant and rave all we want, but it makes no difference unless the message gets across to those who hold the power to make the changes."

"In New York they've been coping with ghettos for years, here they're just beginning. Still, I don't think your kids are quite as badly off."

I shrugged. "Maybe. But it won't be long before they catch up. How much time do you think we have left?"

She shook her head. "About twenty minutes, then I have to get back to work."

We both laughed and finished off the wine.

Priscilla's mother phoned me during the summer to tell me about the growing number of mothers in the community who were organizing themselves to create some kind of recreational program and get a day-care centre going. "We're really pickin up steam. We've felt hopeless for so long it feels good to be gettin somewhere. Maybe we can hang in here for a while longer, and thanks for taking such an interest in Priscilla."

Driving down Yonge Street one hot August day, I heard a familiar voice shouting at me from the curb.

"Sir! Sir!" T.J. was standing on the street corner waving his arms. "Hey, sir! Gimmie a lift!"

I pulled my van over and he hopped in. He asked me to take him to the nearest subway station, pulling a package of cigarettes from his shirt pocket and offering me one.

"Export A's the strongest you can get," he grinned. "It's a real man's brand."

I sighed. "No thanks, T.J. I'm smoking a pipe these days."

"Well, if you need some hash, I can get you the best stuff on the street."

I gave him a friendly scowl and he winked, taking a drag.

"You're such a square, man," he laughed.

When I asked him how his mother was, his face suddenly became serious. "I'm not livin at home," he said. "I'm in a group home now. There's me, four other creeps and two girls. Me and one other guy fuck one of the girls. The other girl is a hose bag—nobody'd ever fuck her! The counsellors there give us spendin money, and I usually buy cigarettes and skin mags."

"Still the same T.J.," I said. "How're your parents?"

"Still separated," he said. "Last time I was at my mother's my dad called up and told her she was a fuckin whore, so I went over to my dad's place and he was so drunk he could hardly stand up. So I beat the shit out of him. I took off my boots and hammered him good. The first shot hit him in the throat with the steel toe—he went right down and didn't get up. I gave him a few more shots in the head and left."

I stopped the van outside the subway.

"Anyway, sir," T.J. concluded, "you don't wanna hear all that shit." He squeezed my arm and jumped out of the van. I called out to him, but he quickly disappeared down the subway entrance.

At the end of August, I took a last walk through the Corridor.

Boisterous, ragged kids ran pell-mell through the dark warrens of the tenements. A fat, ruddy-nosed man leaned over a balcony and cried, "Get your butts outta here!" Women wearing black shawls and carrying shopping bags waited anxiously at the bus stop.

I walked past "St. Welfare" and recalled a conversation I once had with one of the Catholic teachers. She quoted a few lines from the Trappist monk and writer, Thomas Merton: "We refuse to love our neighbours, and excuse ourselves on the premise that society's laws will take care of everything, or that a revolution will solve all our problems."

I finally reached the school and looked in through a

front window. The room was clean, waiting for the new year. I glanced up at the window of my former classroom. Bits of tape were still stuck to the glass, tape that had held the valentines in February. For a moment I thought I saw a kid's face pressed against the glass, but it must have been my imagination. . . .

During quiet walks along the beach on the long, hot nights I remembered good times and bad, and silently made my farewell to my kids.

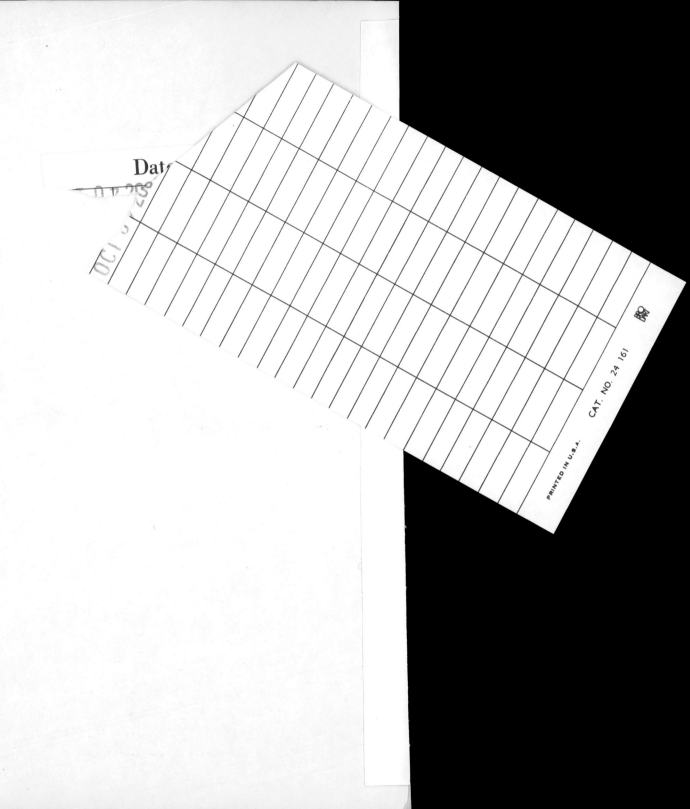

Date

CAT. NO. 24 161

PRINTED IN U.S.A.